P9-CKZ-113

MY PRIZES

MY PRIZES

An Accounting

THOMAS BERNHARD

*Translated from the German
by Carol Brown Janeway*

ALFRED A. KNOPF   NEW YORK   2010

THIS IS A BORZOI BOOK
PUBLISHED BY ALFRED A. KNOPF

Published in the United States by Alfred A. Knopf, a division of
Random House, Inc., New York, and in Canada by Random House of
Canada Limited, Toronto. Originally published in Germany as *Meine
Preise* by Suhrkamp Verlag, Frankfurt am Main, in 2009.
Copyright © 2009 by Suhrkamp Verlag, Frankfurt am Main.

www.aaknopf.com

Library of Congress Cataloging-in-Publication Data
Bernhard, Thomas.
[Meine Preise. English]
My prizes : an accounting / by Thomas Bernhard ; translated from
the German by Carol Brown Janeway.—1st American ed.
p.   cm.
ISBN 978-0-307-27287-4
1. Bernhard, Thomas.   2. Authors, Austrian—20th century—
Biography.   3. Literary prizes.   I. Title.
PT2662.E7Z46 2010
838'. 91409—dc22
[B]
2010015936

Manufactured in the United States of America
First American Edition

Contents

PRIZES

The Grillparzer Prize

For the awarding of the Grillparzer Prize of the Academy of Sciences in Vienna I had to buy a suit, as I had suddenly realized two hours before the presentation that I couldn't appear at this doubtless extraordinary ceremony in trousers and a pullover, and so I had actually made the decision on the so-called Graben to go to the Kohlmarkt and outfit myself with appropriate formality, to which end, based on previous shopping for socks on several occasions, I picked the best-known gentleman's outfitters with the descriptive name Sir Anthony, if I remember correctly it was nine forty-five when I went into Sir Anthony's salon, the award ceremony for the Grillparzer Prize was at eleven, so I had plenty of time. I intended to buy myself the best pure-wool suit in anthracite, even if it was off the peg, with matching socks, a tie, and an Arrow shirt in fine cloth, striped gray and blue. The difficulty of initially making oneself understood in the so-called finer emporiums is well-known, even if the customer immediately says what he's looking for in the most concise terms, at first he'll be stared at incredulously until he repeats what he wants. But naturally the salesman he's talking to hasn't taken it in yet. So it took longer than it need have that time in Sir Anthony to be led to the relevant racks. In fact the arrangement of this shop was already familiar to me from buying socks there and I myself knew better than the salesman where to find the suit I was looking for. I walked over to the rack with the suits in question and pointed to one particular example, which the salesman took down from the rod to hold up for my inspection. I checked the quality of the material and even tried it on in the dressing room. I bent forward several times and leaned back and found that the trousers fit. I put on the jacket, turned around several times in front of the mirror, raised my arms and lowered them again, the jacket fit like the trousers. I walked around the shop in the suit a little bit, and took the opportunity to find the shirt and the socks. Finally I said I would keep the suit on, and I also wanted to put on the shirt and the socks. I found a tie, put it on, tightened it as much as I could, inspected myself once more in the mirror, paid, and went out. They had packed my old trousers and pullover in a bag with "Sir Anthony" on it, so with this bag in my hand, I crossed the Kohlmarkt to meet my aunt, with whom I was going to rendezvous in the Gerstner Restaurant on the Kärnterstrasse, up on the second floor. We wanted to eat a sandwich in order to forestall any malaise or even fainting episode during the proceedings. My aunt had already been to Gerstner's, she had already classified my sartorial transformation as acceptable, and uttered her famous *well, all right.* Until this moment I hadn't worn a suit for years, yes until then I had always appeared in nothing but trousers and pullover, even to the theater if I went at all, I only went in trousers and pullover, mainly in gray wool trousers and a bright red, coarse-knit sheep's-wool pullover that a well-disposed American had given me right after the war. In this outfit, I remember, I had traveled to Venice several times and gone to the famous theater at La Fenice, once to a production of Monteverdi's *Tancredi* directed by Vittorio Gui, and I had been with these trousers and pullover in Rome, in Palermo, in Taormina, and in Florence, and in almost all the other capitals of Europe, apart from the fact that I have almost always worn these articles of clothing at home, the shabbier the trousers and pullover, the more I loved them, for years people only saw me in these trousers and this pullover, I've worn these pieces of clothing for more than a quarter of a century. Suddenly, on the Graben as I said and two hours before the awarding of the Grillparzer Prize, I found these pieces of clothing, which had grown in these decades to be a second skin, to be unsuitable for an honor connected with the name Grillparzer which would take place in the Academy of Sciences. Sitting down in the Gerstner I suddenly had the feeling the trousers were too tight for me, I thought it's probably the way all new trousers feel, and the jacket suddenly felt too tight and also as regards the jacket, I thought this is normal. I ordered a sandwich and drank a glass of beer with it. So who had won this so-called Grillparzer Prize before me, asked my aunt, and for the moment the only name that came to me was Gerhart Hauptmann, I'd read that once and that was the occasion I learned of the existence of the Grillparzer Prize for the first time. The prize is not awarded regularly, only on a *case-by-case* basis, I said, and I thought that it was now

six or seven years between awards, maybe sometimes only five, I didn't know exactly, I still don't
know today. Also this awarding of the prize was naturally making me nervous and I tried to distract
myself and my aunt from the fact that there was
only half an hour before the ceremony began, I
described the outrageousness of my deciding on
the Graben to buy a suit for the ceremony and
that it had been self-evident that I would find the
shop on the Kohlmarkt which stocks English suits
by Chester Barry and Burberry. Why, I had asked
myself again, shouldn't I buy a top-quality suit, even
if it is off the peg, and now the suit I was wearing was a suit made by Barry. My aunt again only
focused on the material and was happy with the
English quality. Again she said her famous *well, all
right.* About the cut, nothing. It was classic. She was
very happy about the fact that the Academy of Sciences was awarding me that Grillparzer Prize today,
she said, and proud, but more happy than proud,
and she got to her feet and I followed her out of the
Gerstner and down onto the street. We had only a
few steps to walk to the Academy of Sciences. The
bag with "Sir Anthony" on it had become deeply
repellent to me, but I couldn't change things. I'll
hand over the bag before going into the Academy of

Sciences, I thought. Some friends who didn't want to miss me being honored were also on their way, we met them in the entrance hall of the Academy. A lot of people were already gathered there and it looked as if the hall was already full. The friends left us in peace and we looked around the hall for some important person to greet us. I walked up and down the entrance hall of the Academy several times with my aunt, but nobody took even the slightest notice of us. So let's go in, I said, and thought, inside the hall some important person will greet me and lead me to the appropriate place with my aunt. Everything in the hall indicated tremendous festiveness and I literally had the sensation that my knees were trembling. My aunt, too, kept looking, as I did, for an important person to greet us. In vain. So we simply stood in the entrance to the hall and waited. But people were pushing past us and kept bumping into us and we had to recognize that we had chosen the least suitable place to wait. Well, is no one going to receive us? we thought. We looked around. The hall was already just about packed and all for the sole purpose of my being awarded the Grillparzer Prize of the Academy of Sciences, I thought. And no one is greeting me and my aunt. At the age of eighty-one she looked wonderful, elegant, intelligent, and in these moments she seemed to be brave as never before. Now various musicians from the Philharmonic had also taken their places at the front of the podium and everything was pointing to the beginning of the ceremony. But not one person had taken any notice of us, who were supposed to be the centerpiece. So I suddenly had an idea: we'll just go in, I said to my aunt, and sit in the middle of the hall where there are still a few free seats, and we'll wait. We went into the hall and found those free seats in the middle of the hall, many people had to stand and complained to us as we forced our way past them. So now we were sitting in the tenth or eleventh row in the middle of the hall of the Academy of Sciences and we waited. All the so-called guests of honor had now taken their places. But of course the ceremony didn't begin. And only I and my aunt knew why. Up front on the podium at ever-decreasing intervals excited gentlemen were running this way and that as if they were looking for something, namely me. The running this way and that by the gentlemen on the podium went on for a while, during which unrest was already breaking out in the hall. In the meantime the Minister for Sciences had arrived and taken her seat in the front row. She was greeted by the President of the Academy, whose name was

Hunger, and led to her chair. A whole line of other so-called dignitaries who were unknown to me were greeted and led to the first or second row. Suddenly I saw a gentleman on the podium whisper something into the ear of another gentleman while simultaneously pointing into the tenth or eleventh row with an outstretched hand, I was the only one who knew he was pointing at me. What happened next is as follows: The gentleman who had whispered something into the ear of the other gentleman and pointed at me went down into the hall and right to my row and made his way along to me. Yes, he said, why are you sitting here when you're the most important person in this celebration and not up front in the first row where we, he actually said we, where we have reserved two places for you and your companion? Yes, why? he asked again and it seemed as if all eyes in the hall were on me and the gentleman. The President, said the gentleman, is asking you please to come to the front, so please come to the front, your seat is right next to the Minister, Herr Bernhard. Yes I said if it's that simple, but naturally I will only go into the first row if President Hunger has requested me *personally* to do so, it goes without saying only if President Hunger is inviting me *personally* to do so. My aunt said nothing during this scene and the guests of the ceremony all looked at us and the gentleman went back along the whole row and then toward the front and whispered something from beside the Minister into President Hunger's ear. After this there was much unrest in the hall, only the tuning-up by the players from the Philharmonic stopped it from becoming something really ugly and I saw that President Hunger was laboriously making his way toward me. Now is the time to stand firm, I thought, demonstrate my intransigence, courage, single-mindedness. I'm not going to go and meet them, I thought, just as (in the deepest sense of the word) they didn't meet me. When President Hunger reached me, he said he was sorry, what he was sorry for, he didn't say. Please would I be kind enough to come with my aunt to the front row, my seat and my aunt's were between the Minister and him. So my aunt and I followed President Hunger into the front row. When we had sat down and an indefinable murmur had spread throughout the hall, the ceremony could begin. I think the men from the Philharmonic played a piece by Mozart. Then there were several longer or shorter speeches about Grillparzer. The one time I glanced over at Minister Firnberg, that was her name, she had fallen asleep, which hadn't escaped President

Hunger either, for the Minister was snoring, even if very quietly, she was snoring, she was snoring the quiet, world-famous ministerial snore. My aunt was following the so-called ceremony with the greatest attention, when some turn of phrase in one of the speeches sounded too stupid or even too comical, she gave me a complicit glance. The two of us were having our own experience. Finally, after about an hour and a half, President Hunger stood up and went to the podium and announced the awarding of the Grillparzer Prize to me. He read out a few words of praise about my work, not without naming some titles of plays that were supposed to be by me but which I hadn't actually written, and listed a row of European famous names who had been singled out for the prize before me. Herr Bernhard was receiving the prize for his play *A Feast for Boris,* said Hunger (the play that had been appallingly badly acted a year before by the Burgtheater company in the Academy Theater), and then, as if to embrace me, he opened his arms wide. The signal for me to step onto the podium had arrived. I stood up and went to Hunger. He shook my hand and gave me a so-called award certificate of a tastelessness, like every other award certificate I have ever received, that was beyond comparison. I hadn't intended to say anything on the podium, I hadn't been asked to do so at all. So in order to choke off my embarrassment, I said a brief *Thank you!* and went back down into the hall and sat down. Whereupon Herr Hunger also sat down and the musicians from the Philharmonic played a piece by Beethoven. While the musicians from the Philharmonic were playing, I thought over the entire ceremony now ending, whose peculiarity and tastelessness and mindlessness naturally had not yet had the chance to register in my consciousness. The musicians from the Philharmonic had barely finished playing when up stood Minister Firnberg and, immediately, President Hunger and both of them went to the podium. Now everyone in the hall had stood up and was pushing toward the podium, toward the Minister naturally and President Hunger who was talking to the Minister. I stood with my aunt, dumbfounded and increasingly at a loss, and we listened to the rising hubbub of a myriad of voices. After a time the Minister looked around and asked in a voice in which inimitable arrogance competed with stupidity: *So, where is the little poet?* I had been standing right next to her but I didn't dare to make myself known. I took my aunt and we left the hall. Unhindered and without a single person having taken any notice of us, we left the Academy of Sciences at around one o'clock. Outside, friends were waiting for us. With these friends, we went to have lunch in the place called the Gösser Bierklinik. A philosopher, an architect, their wives, and my brother. All entertaining people. I no longer remember what we ate. When I was asked during the meal how large the prize money was, it was the first time I really took in the fact that the prize had no money attached to it at all. My own humiliation then struck me as common impudence. But it's one of the greatest honors that can be bestowed on an Austrian, to receive the Grillparzer Prize of the Academy of Sciences, said someone at the table, I think it was the architect. It was huge, said the philosopher. My brother, as always on such occasions, said nothing. After the meal I suddenly had the feeling that the newly bought suit was far too tight and went into the shop on the Kohlmarkt, Sir Anthony I mean, and said to them in a fairly brash way but still with perfect politeness that I wished to exchange the suit, I had just bought the suit, as they knew, but it was at least one size too small. It was my firmness that made the salesman I was speaking to go straight to the rack from which my suit had come. Without objection he let me slip into the same suit but one size larger and I immediately felt that this suit fit. How could I have thought only a few hours ago that the one-size-smaller suit fit me? I clutched my head. Now I was wearing the suit that actually fit and I left the shop with the greatest sense of relief. Whoever buys the suit I have just returned, I thought, has no idea that it's been with me at the awarding of the Grillparzer Prize of the Academy of Sciences in Vienna. It was an absurd thought, and at this absurd thought I took heart. I spent a most enjoyable day with my aunt and we kept laughing over the people at Sir Anthony, who had let me exchange my suit without objections, although I had already worn it to the awarding of the Grillparzer Prize in the Academy of Sciences. That they were so obliging is something about the people in Sir Anthony in the Kohlmarkt that I shall never forget.

The Prize of the Cultural Circle of the
Federal Association of German Industry

In the summer of nineteen seventy-six I spent three months in the Lung Disease Hospital that was and is attached to the Steinhof Insane Asylum in Vienna, in the Hermann Pavilion which had seven rooms with either two or three patients, all of which patients died during the time I was there, with the exception of a theology student and me. I have to mention this because it is quite simply essential for what follows. I had, as so often before, hit the limits of my physical existence once again and the doctors had abandoned me. They'd given me no more than another few months, at best no more than a year, and I accepted my fate. I had been cut open below the larynx for the purposes of the removal of a tissue sample and left for six weeks in the certainty that I was going to die of cancer until they discovered that in my case it pointed to a lifelong lung infection causing an illness called Morbus Boeck, although this hasn't yet been proved and I have lived until this day with that assumption, and, I believe, more intensely than ever. Back then, in the Hermann Pavilion, among the hundred-percent-certain candidates for death I made my peace, just as they did, with my rapidly approaching end. The summer, I remember, was particularly hot and the Six-Day War that had already entered history was raging between Israel and Egypt. The patients lay in bed in the shadows in eighty-six-degree heat and in truth, like me, they were all longing for death and they all, as I have already said, got their wish and died one after the other, among them the former policeman Immervoll who was in the room next to mine and who, for as long as he was in a state to do so, came to my room every single day to play Pontoon with me, he won and I lost, for weeks he won and I lost until he died and I didn't. Both of us passionate Pontoon players, we played Pontoon together to kill time until it wasn't time that was killed, it was he. He died only three hours after playing and winning the last game. In the bed next to mine was a theology student whom in the course of a few weeks hanging between life and death I made into a skeptic and thus a good Catholic, forever, or so I think. I undermined him with my theories about bigoted Catholicism using contemporary examples from the hospital, from the daily course of events with the doctors and nurses and patients, and also from the repellent priests and nuns who buzzed around all over the mental hospital on the scrubby, windy Baumgartner Heights, this westerly range of hills in Vienna, it wasn't hard for me to open the eyes of my pupil. I think his own parents were grateful for my lessons. I gave them with passion, also their son, as I know, did not become a theologian, even if he was a very good Catholic but no theologian, today, I'm sad to say, like everyone else in Central Europe, he's a rather unsuccessful, sidelined, paralyzed socialist. But it gave me the greatest pleasure to explicate the God he had clung to so unconditionally, to literally enlighten him, to rouse the sleeping skeptic in his sickbed, which in turn roused me in my own sickbed and possibly signified my own survival. I am recounting this because when I remember the price of the prize of the Cultural Circle of the Federal Association of German Industry, it all, quite simply, comes back to me, the sweltering hospital in the summer heat, and the hopelessness. I see the patients and their relatives, both with the hopelessness steadily tightening around their throats, the perfidious doctors, the bigoted nurses, all these stunted characters in the stinking, sticky hospital corridors, meanness and hysteria and self-sacrifice in equal measure, deployed only for the purposes of human destruction and I hear in the fall the thousands upon thousands of Russian cranes flying high above the hospital, darkening and blackening the afternoon sky and shattering the eardrums of all the patients with their shrieking cries. I see the squirrels picking up the hundreds of paper handkerchiefs filled with sputum and discarded by the lung patients and racing like mad with them for the trees. I see the famous Professor Salzer coming up from the city to the Baumgartner Heights, and going through the corridors to excise the lobes of the patients' lungs in the operating theater, with his famous little-Professor-Salzer's elegance, the professor was a specialist in larynxes and halves of thoraxes, the professor came increasingly frequently to the Baumgartner Heights and increasing numbers of patients had ever-decreasing numbers of larynxes and thoraxes. I see them all prostrating themselves before Professor Salzer, although the professor couldn't work any miracles and could only cut into the patients and mutilate them with the best of intentions and I see him with his meticulous planning and highly developed skills bringing the victims of his work to an earlier grave than they would have found of their own accord, although he, the best of the best in his field, could do nothing about it, quite the opposite, he and his art and his elegance were totally guided by his high, even the highest, ethics. They all wanted to be operated on by Professor Salzer, who was an uncle of my friend Paul Wittgenstein, one of the expert authorities at the University in the city, and so unapproachable that if they'd been standing in front of him, they'd have lost their voices. The professor's coming, the word went out, and the entire hospital became a holy place. The Six-Day War between Israel and Egypt was at its height, and my aunt, who came to the Baumgartner Heights every day after a two-hour journey in the streetcar in boiling heat carrying several pounds of newspapers, brought me the first copy of *Gargoyles*. But I was too weak to be able to take pleasure in it, even for a moment. My theology student was amazed that I wasn't happy, that I wasn't proud of the beautifully printed book, I couldn't even lift it. My aunt stayed with me all through visiting hours, how often she held the basin under my chin when I vomited after so-called attacks. I lay there with the same incision below the larynx as the people dying to my right and left, and got the news that I had been selected for the so-called prize of the Cultural Circle of the Federal Association of German Industry. I have sketched this more gloomy than entertaining introduction because I want to establish why this so-called prize was more welcome to me back then than anything could have been. Just to be accepted into the hospital—and I had had to be delivered to the hospital on the Baumgartner Heights!—I had first had to pay over the sum of fifteen thousand schillings, which naturally I didn't have and which my aunt advanced to me. But of course I wanted to pay her back this amount as soon as possible, so I had barely been delivered to the hospital on the Baumgartner Heights before I wrote to my publisher about the amount, more accurately to the editor, with the request that my publisher send me two thousand marks. And promptly a few days after my request two thousand marks arrived for me. Then I wrote to my editor that I would thank my publisher immediately for the two thousand marks, but I had barely sent off the letter to the editor before she sent a telegram *Do not thank the publisher!* Why not, I had no idea. I learned *she* had laid out the two thousand marks from her own private bank account, the publisher had been unwilling. It is depressing to have to get hold of fifteen thousand schillings just to be admitted to a death ward, but that is how things were, those were the circumstances. In brief, this was the situation into which the news arrived that I should expect the prize of the Cultural Circle of the Federal Association of German Industry. The award event would take place in the fall, either September or October, I no longer remember. In any case, I had been out of the hospital for a mere two or three days before traveling to Regensburg, where they planned to stage the award ceremony in the town hall. The poet Elisabeth Borchers was due to share the award with me. I went to Regensburg weak-kneed, with a shoulderbag of my grandfather's. All the way up the Danube, I thought of nothing but the eight thousand marks, the gigantic sum of money I was to receive. I dreamed of the eight thousand marks behind closed eyes and painted the scene that awaited me in Regensburg. I was to be put up at the Hotel Thurn und Taxis, a famous address. My frailty made me keep dozing off at the compartment window the whole way along, the Danube, the Gothic, the German Emperors, I kept thinking, but whenever I woke up from my dozes the first thing I thought about was always the eight thousand marks. I didn't know Herr Rudolf de la Roi, the spokesman of the Cultural Circle of the Federal Association of German Industry, who had given me the award. Probably, I thought, he knows about my illness and because of my illness he has made sure I got the prize. This thought lowered my self-estimation, for I would like to have received the award for *Gargoyles* or for *Frost,* not for *Morbus Boeck.* But I must not brood, I forbade myself to devalue this award even before I'd received it. Doderer and Gütersloh have received this award before you, I thought, writers of major stature, even if I had no access to them, nor could. Three days ago still in your sickbed, now already en route to Regensburg where the Gothic awaits you, I thought. The Danube kept getting narrower, the landscape kept getting more lovely, finally, as it suddenly turned desolate and gray and insipid, there was Regensburg. I got out and went straight to the Hotel Thurn und Taxis. It really was a first-class hotel for a town like Regensburg. I liked it and I truly did immediately feel well in this hotel, and from the very first moment, I wasn't alone, but in the company of Elisabeth Borchers, whom I had already met in Luxembourg at one of the many so-called Poets' Assemblies to which I used to go with my poems when I was around twenty. So there was none of the boredom that always hits me otherwise in every hotel in the entire world where I arrive on my own. I knew that Borchers was an intelligent person and a charming lady and her reputation in my eyes was superb. We wound our way through the town, laughing madly, and used the opportunity to enjoy a casual evening together. Naturally it didn't run late, my illness soon sent me to bed. The next day I met Herr Rudolf de le Roi and the publisher of *Akzente,* Hans Bender, who, I assume, had a say in the awarding of the prize, I still have a photograph of Borchers and Bender in front of a Gothic Regensburg fountain. I didn't like the town. It's cold and repulsive and if I hadn't had Borchers and my thoughts of the eight thousand marks, I would probably have left again after the first hour. How I hate these medium-sized towns with their famous historical buildings by which their inhabitants allow themselves to be perverted their whole lives long. Churches and narrow alleys in which people vegetate, their minds turning more mindless all the time. Salzburg, Augsburg, Regensburg, Würzburg, I hate them all, because mindlessness has been kept warming over in them for hundreds of years. But I kept going back to the eight thousand marks. During my Morbus Boeck illness so many debts mounted up that I can now pay off, I thought. And at the end there'll still be an amount left over just for me. So I let the morning of the ceremonial awarding of the prize of the Cultural Circle of the Federal Association of German Industry (naturally I want to be sure I always use the full, correct title) creep up on me. Herr de la Roi collected me and Frau Borchers and we went to the town hall, which ranks as one of the precious monuments of German Gothic. It threatened to stifle and choke me as soon as I went in, but I said to myself, Be brave, be brave, just be brave, go along with everything that's going to happen and take the check for eight thousand marks and vanish. The ceremony was fairly short. Herr von Bohlen und Halbach, the Chairman of the Federal Association of German Industry, was to make the presentation to Frau Borchers and myself. We had taken our seats in the front row with Doctor de le Roi. To the left and right of us were the town dignitaries including the mayor wearing his heavy chain of office. I had eaten too much the night before and felt queasy. I can no longer remember whether there was a speech, but probably there was, for such cere-

monies always have to include a speech. The guests
of honor threatened to cause the main room in the
town hall to explode. I could hardly breathe. I was
in danger of suffocating in the air of the hall. Everything was all sweat and dignity. But we'd laughed
so much the night before, I thought, Frau Borchers
and I, that it was all worth it for that alone. And now
the eight thousand marks on top of it all! In a
moment all the magic rigmarole will be over and
we'll have the checks in our hands! I thought. Of
course a chamber music ensemble had also taken
their seats here too, what they played escapes me.
And then, as I recall, the definitive moment arrived
without warning. President von Bohlen und Halbach stepped to the podium and read from a piece of
paper the following: . . . *and the Federal Association
of German Industry herewith bestows the nineteen
sixty-seven awards on Frau Bernhard and Herr
Borchers!* My neighbor jumped, as I noticed. She
was in shock for a second. I squeezed her hand and
told her she should just think about the money,
whether it was Herr Borchers and Frau Bernhard or
Herr Bernhard and Frau Borchers, as was the fact,
was irrelevant. Frau Borchers and I got up on the
stage of the Regensburg town hall, in which absolutely nobody aside from those affected and perhaps

also Herr de le Roi and Herr Bender had noticed Herr von Bohlen und Halbach's mistake, and we each received a check for eight thousand marks. We also spent a beautiful day in the horrible town and I returned to Vienna where I was welcomed and fussed over by my aunt. A year ago I received a so-called Jubilee Book from the Cultural Circle of the Federal Association of German Industry, the so-called *Jahresring*, which proudly presents all of their prizewinners. My name was the only one missing. Had Doctor de le Roi, the extremely nice (as I recall) gentleman, removed my name from the list of honorees because of the changes in my life meantime, changes I find no fault with myself? In any case, here I have the opportunity to share with you the fact that I too am a winner of the prize of the Cultural Circle of the Federal Association of German Industry. And in Regensburg. And in the town hall in Regensburg to boot.

The Literature Prize of the
Free Hanseatic City of Bremen

After five blank years, when I wrote *Frost* in Vienna in twelve months (1962), my future was bleaker than it had ever been. I had sent *Frost* to a friend, who was an editor at the Insel publishing house, and the manuscript was accepted within three days. But even as it was accepted, I realized that my work was incomplete and could not be published with its current defects. In a boardinghouse in Frankfurt which was on one of the busiest streets near the Eschenheimer Tower and was one of the cheapest I could consider, I revised the entire book, and all the sections in *Frost* that have a title as a heading, I wrote in that boardinghouse. I got up at five in the morning and sat at the little table in the window and when by midday I had written five or eight or even ten pages, I would take them and run to my editor at Insel to go over with her where these pages had to be slotted into the manuscript. The entire book was transformed during those weeks in Frankfurt, I threw away many pages, probably around a hundred, until it seemed to be acceptable and could go into production. When the galleys came, I was on a trip to Warsaw to visit a girlfriend who was studying at the Academy of Art there. I took a room at the coldest time of year in the so-called Dziekanka, a student residence right near the palace headquarters of the regime, ran around for weeks in the beautiful, exciting, eerie city of Warsaw, and read the galleys. At lunchtime I ate in the so-called Writers' Club and in the evenings with the actors, where the food was even better. I spent one of the happiest times of my life in Warsaw, I had the galleys in the pocket of my coat, my chief interlocutor was Lec the satirist who wrote his famous aphorisms in his wife's kitchen notebook and often invited me home and sometimes also bought me a coffee on the Nowy Âwiat. I was happy with my book, which came out in the spring of sixty-three along with a review by Zuckmayer that ran for pages in *Die Zeit*. But when the general storm of coverage was over, unusually intense and full of controversy, ranging from the most embarrassing effusions to the most vicious attacks, I was suddenly utterly undone, as if I'd fallen into a pit of terrible despair. I thought I would choke on the error of believing that literature was my hope. I didn't want anything more to do with literature. It hadn't brought me happiness, it had trampled me down into that stifling, stinking pit from which there is no escape, or so I believed. I cursed literature and my prostituting myself with her, and went to work on building sites and took a job as a truck driver with the Christophorus Company in the Klosterneuburgerstrasse. For months I made beer deliveries for the famous Gösser brewery. In the course of this I not only learned to drive trucks very well but I also got to know the city of Vienna even better than I'd known it before. I lived with my aunt and earned my living as a truck driver. I didn't want anything to do with literature anymore, I had put everything I had into literature and literature responded by throwing me into the pit. Literature turned my stomach, I hated all publishers and all publishing houses and all books. It seemed to me that in writing *Frost* I had fallen victim to an enormous fraud. I was happy to let my leather jacket drop onto the driver's seat and go thundering through the streets in the old Steyrer truck. Now it was clear how good it had been to learn to drive a truck all those years ago in preparation for a job in Africa I had wanted to take back then, but which, as I know now, very fortunately never came to anything. But naturally even the good fortune of being able to work as a driver for the Gösser brewery also came to an end. Suddenly I hated what I was doing and gave it up from one day to the next and buried myself under the covers in my little closet at my aunt's. She had understood the state I was in, for one day she invited me to go with her to the mountains for a few months. It would do us both good to discard the sheer grisliness and harmfulness of the big city for some weeks, and give ourselves over to nature. Her goal was Sankt Veit in the Salzburg area, the place near the hospital where I had been a patient for years, twenty-five hundred feet up and an absolutely ideal place for us to recuperate. Early one morning we began our mountain journey from the Westbahnhof, my aunt and I, her all-expenses-paid companion. But I have to say that when the train pulled out of the Westbahnhof I was already cursing the countryside and longing to be back in the city of Vienna. The further the train got from Vienna, the sadder I got, I'm making a mistake, I thought, turning my back on Vienna and going to the countryside with my aunt, but I can no longer correct this mistake. I'm not a country person, I'm a city person, I said to myself, and there was no way back. Naturally I'd never found happiness in the country, the people bored me, I really despised them, nature bored me and I despised nature, I was starting to hate people and nature. I had become gloomy and a brooder, who walked through and around the fields in this direction and that, ran through the woods with my head down, and finally refused all food. Thus it was that my secret opposition to life on the land and in the mountains was leading straight to catastrophe, I was still chained to a truly pitiful caricature of myself and my bottomless existential despair, when the Literature Prize of the Free Hanseatic City of Bremen came. It was not the prize itself that saved me from my emotional, indeed my existential catastrophe, it was the thought that the prize money of ten thousand marks would enable me to get my life under control, give it a radical new direction, make it possible again. The prize was announced, the amount of the prize was known to me already. I had the chance to do the most sensible thing with the money. It had always been my wish to have a house to myself, and even if not a proper house, at least walls around me within which I can do what I want, permit what I want, lock myself in if I want. So I thought, I'll use the prize money to get these walls and I made contact with a real estate agent who immediately came to see me in Sankt Veit and proposed various properties to me. Naturally all these properties were too expensive, if I had the prize money in hand, it would only be a fraction of the sale price. But why not? I thought and I agreed with the real estate agent to meet in January in Upper Austria where he lived and had his range of properties to hand, mainly old farmhouses, some of them already partly derelict, all in the price range of between one hundred thousand and two hundred thousand schillings. But my price was nothing over seventy thousand. Maybe for seventy thousand I'd be able to find the right set of walls I can lock myself up in, I wasn't thinking about a house when I thought about a property for myself, I thought about walls and I thought about walls in which I could lock myself up. I went to Upper Austria and my aunt came with me and we visited the real estate agent. The man impressed me, I immediately took a liking to him, he was capable and seemed to have no character flaws. We came out into a landscape where the snow lay more than three feet deep and stamped our way to the real estate agent's house. He put us into his car and explained by way of a piece of paper where the properties to be visited were situated and what route we should take to get from one property to the next. He had listed about eleven or twelve farms on his paper that were ready to be sold. He slammed the car doors and the tour of inspection had begun. Thick fog already hung over the entire landscape and we saw nothing, we didn't even see the road along which the real estate agent was driving us to the first property. He himself saw nothing ahead of him but fog, but he knew the road and we put ourselves in his hands. My aunt was as curious as I was, we were both silent, I don't know what was going on inside her, she didn't know what was going on inside me, the real estate agent didn't know what was going on inside us both, he didn't say a single word, came to a sudden stop and indicated that we were to get out. And I actually saw a huge wall in front of me in the fog, built of great blocks of stone. The real estate agent moved a large gate that had been torn off its hinges and we went into a big farmyard. There was also more than three feet of snow in the farmyard, it looked as if the owners of the property had departed in a rush, leaving everything lying or standing where it was, I thought: the owners have met with some great misfortune. The property had been standing empty for a year, said the real estate agent, and went ahead of us. In every room we stepped into, he said this was a particularly beautiful room and he kept repeating the two words *exceptional proportions* and it didn't bother him in the slightest that at every moment he was putting a foot through one of the rotted floors and had to rescue himself from the depths of the rot with a well-executed jump. The real estate agent led the way. I followed behind him and my aunt behind me. We went through the rooms as if we were walking along planks that we needed to cross some dull fetid pond, sometimes I looked around for my aunt, who turned out however to be very agile, more agile than me and the real estate agent. There were eleven or twelve rooms to inspect, all of them in totally dilapidated condition and the smell of hundreds if not thousands, I thought, of desiccated ancient mice and rats filled the air. All the floors were rotted through, completely punky and most of the window frames had been torn out by the wind or the weather. Down in the kitchen, where there was a large rusting enameled stove encrusted in dirt, the water had not been turned off and water was running onto the floor and under the floor and the real estate agent said the owners, who'd left the house a year ago, had forgotten to turn off the tap and he went over to the tap and turned it off. He himself, he said, had never inspected the property before this, we were the first he'd shown it to, he was enchanted by the exceptional proportions. My aunt held a handkerchief in front of her mouth to block the stench that pervaded the property, not only the smell of rot, the stalls were full of enormous heaps of manure which the owners had not cleared away. The real estate agent kept saying *exceptional proportions* and the more often he asserted this, the clearer it became to me that he was right, in the end it wasn't *him* saying the property had exceptional proportions, it was *me* saying it, and saying it at every moment. I kept working myself up to say *exceptional proportions* at briefer and briefer intervals until finally I was convinced that the entire property really did have *exceptional proportions.* From one moment to the next, I had been possessed by the entire property and when we were outside the gate again, to drive to the next one and the real estate agent was now hurrying, for we still had ten or twelve properties ahead of us to be inspected, I said that all these properties no longer interested me, I had already found the property for me; it was this one, for it had truly *exceptional pro-portions,* they were ideal for me and I wished to con-clude the requisite contract with the real estate agent immediately. From the start of our inspection to this statement of mine, no more than fifteen min-utes had passed. My aunt was shocked, she said I mustn't do anything crazy, she found these walls horrible, naturally, and when we were in the car again, driving back to the real estate agent's house to set up the contract, she kept saying from behind me that I should think the whole thing over carefully, *sleep on it,* she said. But my decision was unbudge-able. I had found my walls. I proposed to the real estate agent that I make a down payment of seventy thousand schillings at the end of January, i.e., after the prize ceremony in Bremen, and settle the remainder of the balance in the course of the year. All the same this remainder amounted to one hun-dred and fifty thousand schillings, and if I had absolutely no idea yet where this money would come from, I had absolutely no worries about it. *Think it over, sleep on it,* my aunt kept saying while the real estate agent was already drawing up the contract. I liked the real estate agent's manner, the way he wrote, what he said, his surroundings. I myself behaved as if money played no role, it impressed the real estate agent while his wife was making a delicious egg dish for us in the kitchen. Half an hour after I had seen Nathal, that was the name of my walls, for the first time, and not even seen them clearly, for as I've already said they were wrapped in fog, and quite apart from the fact that I had seen absolutely nothing of what surrounded the walls, i.e., the landscape, only made conjectures, I signed the so-called preliminary contract. We ate the egg dish and talked for awhile with the real estate agent and left him. He brought us to the train and we went back to the mountains. During the journey, my aunt didn't miss a single word in expressing her worst premonitions, and I admit I got the willies, now I was suddenly thinking about what had actually just happened, for I had of course got myself into a nightmare. I spent a series of sleepless nights during which I failed naturally to come to grips with what I had really done and what I'd signed and where I would find the so-called balance of one hundred and fifty thousand schillings. But the day of the prize-giving in Bremen will come and then I'll have the first seventy-thousand-schilling installment and I'm saved, I thought. My aunt refrained from any comment whatsoever. For the first time in our lives together I had failed to listen to her advice. So I traveled to Bremen, which I didn't know. Hamburg I knew and loved as I do still today, Bremen I loathed from the very first moment, it's a petit bourgeois, unbelievably sterile city. A room had been reserved for me in a newly built hotel directly opposite the station, I no longer remember its name. I hid in my hotel room so as not to have to see the city of Bremen, waited for morning and the prize-giving. This prize-giving was to take place in Bremen's old town hall and that is where it did. My biggest problem was that I had been instructed to give a speech to the audience and I was already in Bremen and didn't yet have the beginnings of an idea for such a speech, which I'd known about for weeks, and even during the night no idea for such a speech came to me and in the morning I still had none. But now it was getting urgent. During breakfast I remembered that one thing about Bremen is Grimm's "Bremen Town Musicians," and I made up a concept with the Bremen Town Musicians as the centerpiece. I finished my tea and ran to my room and sat down on my bed and did a quick draft. I made a second draft and a third. Then I had to admit to myself that my idea had been a bad one and I needed to come up with another. But time was short. In the meantime there had already been phone calls and questions about how long my speech would be. It's not long, I said into the telephone, not long at all, I said, although I still didn't have even an idea for such a speech. Half an hour before the start of the ceremony in the town hall I sat down on my bed and wrote the sentence "In the cold, clarity increases," I thought: now I have an acceptable idea for my speech to the audience. With this as the center, some further sentences developed, and within ten or fifteen minutes I had written at least half a page. When they collected me from the hotel to take me to the town hall, I had just finished my speech. In the cold, clarity increases, I thought as several gentlemen were escorting me to the town hall, I had the feeling they were taking me away to a trial. They had positioned their prisoner in the middle and had advanced from hotel to city to town hall. The town hall was already full, most of all it was full of schoolchildren. This town hall in Bremen is also a famous town hall, but this town hall also depressed me just as all other famous town halls have also depressed me. Here too medals sparkled and the mayoral chains of office glinted. Then I was led ceremoniously into the first row and had to sit next to the mayor. A man stepped up to the podium and talked about me. He spoke very emphatically and it was full of praise, as far as I

recall, but I didn't understand it all. What I was seeing the whole time was my walls in Nathal and what
I was thinking was how to pay for these walls. May
it all be long-drawn-out enough, I thought, for the
money finally to be real liquid cash. When my eulo-
gist had finished and the schoolchildren, or so it
seemed, clapped the most enthusiastically of all, I
was signaled to go up to the podium. On the podium
the prize was then presented to me, and I no longer
remember what it looked like, I no longer have it,
just as I no longer have any of the other prize docu-
ments, they have gotten lost over the years. Now I
had the document and the check in my hand and
I went to the lectern and read out my notes on the
clarity that increases in the cold. Just as the audience
was beginning to prepare for my speech, it was
already over. That was the shortest speech a Bremen
prizewinner has ever given, I thought, and after the
ceremony this was confirmed to me. So there I stood
and had to shake hands with the mayor again for
the photographers. Outside in the corridor my old
friend the editor suddenly appeared totally unex-
pectedly, the one who had accepted *Frost* within
three days, and said, knowing himself to be totally
alone with me, confidentially so to speak: Please
lend me five thousand marks, I need them desper-

ately. Yes of course, I said, without thinking through the consequences, and I said as soon as it's two o'clock and the banks in Bremen are open again, I'll go to a bank with you and cash the check and give you the five thousand marks. How often he's lent me money, I thought, again and again and again and it wasn't long ago that he rescued me out of one of my fatal financial catastrophes. Immediately after the ceremony there was a lunch in a prominent Bremen restaurant, which I left at two o'clock to go with my friend to the bank and cash the check for *Frost*. Anyhow, I thought, I'm going to Giessen after Bremen to give a reading in a so-called evangelical educational institute and I'll be paid two thousand marks. That'll give me seven thousand marks again. This thought immediately made me happy again. The next day I visited another friend in Bremen who lived there in an attic room and with whom I had a terrific conversation about theater over good tea and a view over the pewter-colored river Weser, most of all we talked about Artaud. Right after this conversation I went back to Vienna. And of course I could no longer expect to move into my newly purchased walls in Nathal. How I eventually got control of it and altered and rebuilt it more or less with my own hands and financed it all over the course of the years doesn't belong here. But the Bremen prize was the impetus for my walls, without it everything would probably have taken a different turn for me and unfolded in another way. In any case I made a second trip to Bremen in connection with the so-called Bremen Literature Prize and I don't want to conceal what happened to me on this second trip to Bremen. I was a so-called member of the jury to select the next prizewinner and I had gone to Bremen with my mind already made up that I would vote for Canetti who, I believe, had not until that time received a single literary award. For whatever reason, anyone but Canetti was out of the question for me, I considered any other choice to be risible. There was this long table, I believe, in a Bremen restaurant where the jury was meeting, and sitting at it was a whole row of gentlemen who were the so-called voting jurors, among them the famous Senator Harmsen, with whom I had a very warm relationship. I think they had all named their own candidates, none of whom was Canetti, when it came to my turn and I said, *Canetti.* I wanted to give Canetti the prize for *Auto-da-Fé,* the brilliant work of his youth which had been reissued a year before this jury met. Several times I said the word *Canetti* and each time the faces around the long table grimaced in a self-pitying sort of way. Many of the people at the table didn't even know who Canetti was, but among the few who did know about Canetti was one who suddenly said, after I had said *Canetti* again, but he's *also* a Jew. Then there was some murmuring, and Canetti landed under the table. I can still hear this phrase *but he's also a Jew* although I can't remember who at the table said it. But even today I often hear the phrase, it came from some really sinister quarter, even if I don't know who said it. This phrase nipped any further debate over my proposal to award Canetti the prize right in the bud. I preferred to take no further part in the discussions and just sat silently at the table. But time was passing quickly and although an endless series of appalling names had been proposed in the meantime, all of which I could only associate with prattling dilettantism, no prizewinner had surfaced yet. The gentlemen were looking at the clock and the smell of the evening's roast was already seeping through the double doors. So the table simply *had* to come to a decision. To my utter amazement one of the gentlemen, again I no longer remember who, regardless of a vote, suddenly pulled a book by Hildesheimer out of the mound of books on the table, and as he was already getting to his feet to leave the lunch, said in a disconcertingly naïve tone: *So let's take Hildesheimer, let's take Hildesheimer,* and Hildesheimer was the one name that had not been uttered in all the hours of discussion. Now suddenly the name Hildesheimer had been uttered and they all shifted in their chairs and were relieved and agreed about Hildesheimer and within a matter of minutes Hildesheimer was voted the new winner of the Bremen prize. Who Hildesheimer really was, not one of them seemed to know. In a moment the news had been passed to the press that after a more-than-two-hour meeting, Hildesheimer was the new prizewinner. The gentlemen stood up and went out into the dining room. The Jew Hildesheimer had won the prize. For me *that* was the point of the prize. I've never been able to keep quiet about it.

The Julius Campe Prize

In nineteen sixty-four the Julius Campe Prize, which the Hamburg publishers Hoffmann und Campe had funded in honor of Heine's publisher Julius Campe, was split three ways and the prize money of fifteen thousand marks went to Gisela Elsner, Hubert Fichte, and me. It was the first time I was singled out for my work as a writer and above all I was enchanted that the distinction came from Hamburg and is indissolubly linked with Heinrich Heine's first publisher, for Julius Campe was the first publisher of *The Harz Journey* and a whole series of the best of all the poems that a German poet has ever written. Julius Campe was not of course unknown to me, I had read Brienitzer's biography of him. In truth the Julius Campe Prize of nineteen sixty-four was not awarded at all because the jury couldn't agree on any one writer and the three equal shares of the prize money were described as so-called Work Stipendiums, but from that moment on, because I had such a stipendium in mind, this didn't hinder me at all from thinking and saying that I'd received the Julius Campe Prize. I was very proud and probably for the only time in my life unequivocally happy to the bottom of my heart about an honor that came in this news from Hamburg and I tried to spread it around as fast as possible. I was living with my aunt in Vienna and I walked through the First District across the Graben and along the Kärntnerstrasse and across the Kohlmarkt and through the Volksgarten and I thought everyone who met me knew of my happiness at having won the Julius Campe Prize. When I sat down at a table differently from before, I held the newspapers in my hand differently from before, and secretly I wondered to myself why everybody in the street hadn't remarked on it to me. And anyone who failed to ask me about it was enlightened by me about my having just won the Julius Campe Prize and I explained who Julius Campe was, which nobody in Vienna knew, and who Heinrich Heine was, for not a lot of people in Vienna knew that either, and what an exceptional honor it was. It's an enormous honor, I said, to receive a prize that's connected with the name of Heinrich Heine and also comes from Hamburg, the city I loved most at that time and has always been one of my favorite cities, even today I know of no other through which I can walk with such uninhibited and happy self-confidence. And in which I could actually live for long intervals, even, who knows, maybe even years. I came to Hamburg very early in my life and maybe it has to do with the fact that I spent the year after I was born on a fishing cutter in Rotterdam harbor that Hamburg was for me what is known in the vernacular as love at first sight. I was often, almost yearly, a guest in a brick house in Wellingsbüttel, not far from the source of the Alster, and I love the people of Hamburg into the bargain. The way the news of my participation in the Julius Campe Prize was announced to me was also, I can say, completely appealing. They wrote two or three sentences that they'd selected me for one of three portions of the prize and I could collect the five thousand marks whenever I wanted, they'd be ready for me in the Hoffmann und Campe offices on the Harvester-huder Weg. There would be no ceremony, no event. So I actually had a good reason to go to Hamburg again, one day I went to the Westbahnhof and got on a train to Copenhagen and found what seemed the best compartment for me to lean back in and go to sleep. But going to sleep was out of the question because my excitement at being singled out for my work as a writer, for *Frost,* was too great. I got the prize from Hamburg, from Hamburg, from Hamburg, I kept thinking, and I secretly despised the Austrians who had not, until now, extended me even a trace of recognition. The news had come down from the north, from the Binnenalster! Hamburg now was not only the most beautiful of great cities to me but also the pinnacle of clear-sightedness, quite apart from the immense cosmopolitanism that has distinguished Hamburg from time immemorial. In Hamburg the Hoffmann und Campe people had reserved a big room for me in an old villa on the Binnenalster, and I had a taxi take me there. I had hardly reached the room before a newspaper called, wanting to interview me. I leaned back in an armchair and said yes. I unpacked my few things and already the phone rang and the people from the newspaper were there and had pulled out their pencils. It was the first interview I ever gave in my life, it's possible I gave it to the *Hamburger Abendblatt,* who knows. I was so excited that I couldn't finish a single sentence, I immediately had an answer for every question but I wasn't happy with my skill in phrasing things. I thought: people are noticing you come from Austria, the back of beyond. The next day I saw my picture in the paper and instead of being on top of the world, as I'd expected, I was ashamed of the nonsense I'd talked to the people from the newspaper when I was giving it my best shot and I loathed my photograph, if I really look like I do in this photograph, I thought, it would be better for me to retreat into some dark valley deep in the mountains and never set foot in the world again. I sat there spreading a thick layer of marmalade on my breakfast bread and felt deeply wounded. I didn't dare even open the curtains and spent several hours sitting in my armchair as if stricken by some indefinable paralysis in my whole body. I felt worse than I'd ever felt before. But suddenly I thought of my share of the prize, the five thousand marks suddenly dominated my mind, and I slipped into my jacket and ran to the offices of Hoffmann und Campe, it was a beautiful walk in the best air and I felt I was seeing the elegant world for the first time in my life. I looked at each of the comfortable villas on the Binnenalster with the greatest interest and the greatest attention. Finally I reached the offices of

Hoffmann und Campe. I announced myself and was immediately welcomed by the head of the house in person. The gentleman shook my hand, invited me to sit down, and took an envelope that was already prepared out of the open desk drawer and handed it to me. The check, he said. Then he asked me if the place I was staying was comfortable. Then there was a pause, during which I kept thinking I should say something clever, something philosophical, or at least something sensible perhaps, but I said nothing, my mouth didn't open. Finally I got the sense that the situation had become embarrassing and right at this point the gentleman said I must come and have lunch with him in the so-called English Club. And I went there for lunch with the gentleman, and ate one of the most outstanding meals I'd ever eaten until then. The meal ended with a generous shot of Fernet Branca and then I was standing in the street on the Alsterufer, and had already said goodbye to the head of Hoffmann und Campe. The main reason for my trip to Hamburg was herewith at an end. I spent another night in the old villa on the Alster and then went to Wellingsbüttel to my friends. I no longer know how long I stayed there. Now I was a famous person, said my friends, and if they went to visit people with me, they said to their hosts, this

Austrian we brought with us is now a famous person. These people all made it hard for me to say goodbye to Hamburg. When I arrived in Vienna, I immediately made good on the decision I'd already reached on the journey to Hamburg: I used the entire amount of the prize to buy myself a car. The purchase of the car happened in the following way: In the display room of the car dealer Heller opposite the so-called Heinrichshof, surrounded by other luxury cars, I saw a Triumph Herald. It was brilliant white and upholstered in red leather. Its dashboard was made of wood with black buttons and its price was exactly thirty-five thousand schillings, i.e., five thousand marks. It was the first car I'd seen on my reconnoitering expedition to look for cars and it was the one I immediately bought. I spent around half an hour in total, coming and going in front of the showroom and looking at the car. It was elegant, it was English, which was already almost a given, and it was exactly the size that suited me. Finally I entered the showroom and went up to the car and walked around the car several times and said, I'm going to buy this car. Yes, said the salesman, he would arrange for a similar car to be delivered for me in the next few days. No, I said, not in the next few days, now, I said, right away. I said *right away* the way I've always said it, very firmly. I am not going to wait for a few days, I said, I can't, I didn't give any reason why, but I said I absolutely couldn't and I said this is the only car I will buy, as is, standing right here. I was making as if to go, without closing the deal, when the salesman suddenly said all right you can have the car, this one, it's a beautiful car. He said it with sadness in his voice but he was right, the car was beautiful. Now I myself, as was flashing through my mind at that moment, had never driven a motorcar in my life before, only heavy trucks, for I had originally taken the truck driver's test because I wanted to go to Africa to deliver medicines to the Africans, but this fell through, driving heavy trucks was a requirement for my job in Africa, I was supposed to go to Ghana, but because of the death of the American manager who would have been my boss my job in Africa got postponed and finally made redundant, so, I thought, I don't have any idea how to drive the car out of the showroom. Yes, I said to the salesman, it's a done deal, I will buy the car but it has to be parked out front for me, in front of the showroom, I said, I would pick it up in the course of the day. Of course, said the salesman. I signed a contract and paid the purchase price. The entire Julius Campe Prize went on it. I had a little money left over for gas. For a few hours I crisscrossed the inner city in jubilation over owning a car, the first car in my life, and what a car! I congratulated myself on my taste. That I should have asked even one person for expert advice on whether the car was worth something under the hood never crossed my mind. I have a car! I have a white car! I thought. Finally I turned around and went back to the Heller dealership, which was one of the most elegant car dealers in Vienna, and when I came around the corner my car was already standing in front of the door. I collected my papers inside, got into the car, and drove off. In the event I had no difficulty steering the car, although it would incontrovertibly have been easier to steer heavy trucks than this little Triumph Herald. Now of course I drove to the Obkirchergasse and showed the car to my aunt. She was absolutely amazed that such an elegant car could be bought for five thousand marks. On the other hand, five thousand marks was an awful lot of money! Of course I couldn't rest in peace until I made my first major trip, which took me first to the north across the Danube and then, because I couldn't get enough, by way of Hollabrunn all the way to Retz. In Retz I'd already used up a lot of gas. I filled up the tank and drove back, it was a beautiful day. But when I was back and in the vicinity of the Obkirchergasse, I didn't want to stop and get out and so I now drove east. First I drove through the entire city and then out into the Burgenland. Shortly before Eisenstadt it began to get dark and I thought if I keep driving I'll be in Hungary in half an hour. I drove back. During the night sleep was not even to be thought of, it was a wonderful feeling to own a car, and an English car what's more, white, with red leather seats and a wooden dashboard. And all that for *Frost,* I thought. The next day I took my aunt on an outing to Klosterneuburg and on the way we stopped at the cemetery in Grinzing. Two months later, I'd accustomed myself to being a car owner and trips in my Herald were already becoming normal, I drove to Istria and the coast of Lovran where my aunt had already gone to stay several weeks before. We were living as so often before in the Villa Eugenia, a villa of the gentry built in 1880 with splendid broad balconies and a pebbled path that curved gently directly down to the deep blue water. Gagarin had just completed his first space flight, I still remember. My white Herald was parked downstairs next to the gateway, it was no gate, it was a gateway and upstairs on the third floor, as the sole master of three large rooms with six large windows behind whisper-thin silk curtains that dated from before the war, I wrote *Amras*. When I'd finished *Amras,* I immediately sent it to my editor at Insel. Four or five days after dispatching *Amras* I was already up at three in the morning with a rush of energy, a feeling I had to head out, up and out, for it was a perfectly cloudless, clear, tangy day. Wearing only trousers and gym shoes and a sleeveless shirt, I climbed the rocky slopes of the so-called Monte Maggiore, now named Učka. Halfway up I lay down in the shade and looked at the sea in front of me, far below, crisscrossed by ships. I had never been happier. At midday, when I ran down the mountain again, laughing aloud, exhausted with happiness, I can say I felt once again that I wouldn't change places with anyone in the world. In the Eugenia there was a telegram waiting for me. *Amras outstanding, everything fine,* was the text. I changed clothes and got into my car and drove into Rijeka, the ancient Croatian-Hungarian port town. I walked all around the little streets and I was quite unbothered by how gray all the people were, unbothered by the pollution in the air from hundreds of cars. I absorbed everything with the utmost intensity, I listened to everything, breathed everything in. Around five in the afternoon I drove back to Eugenia, the coast road, past the shipyards. I think I sang. Before Opatija, where the great rock face catches the harsh light of the evening sun, a car swung into my lane from the left, slamming heavily into the near side of my car and staving it in. It hurled me right out of the car but I just stood there and didn't feel any pain. The car belonging to the Yugoslavian was completely demolished too. The driver had jumped out and run off screaming, pursued by a woman who kept screaming *Idiota! Idiota! Idiota!* after him. There was a pile of metal in front of me in the middle of the road and all the traffic coming out of the shipyards was blocked. The *Idiota! Idiota! Idiota!* faded away and I was standing there alone. Suddenly I saw people running toward me and screaming and I saw that my whole body was covered in blood. I had a head wound, the bleeding was so severe I thought I'd lost my scalp, but I still felt no pain whatever. Then someone who'd leapt out of a little Fiat 500 grabbed hold of me and put me in his car. He gunned the engine and raced me along the coast road to the hospital and he raced so incredibly fast that I thought this was when the real accident would happen. During this whole race I kept holding my head because I thought all the blood would pour right out of it. I also had the feeling I should at least write down my name on a piece of paper, for otherwise no one would know who was involved if I did actually bleed to death. And of course I also didn't want to dirty the man's car with my blood and I tried to keep directing the blood flow just onto me and between my knees. Soon I'm going to lose consciousness, I thought, and then that will be that. Once at the hospital, I was immediately put flat on a gurney by a nurse and taken away. In a washroom the nurse shaved half my skull. Then I immediately found myself in an operating room and I was in luck, for the surgeon spoke German and promptly asked me all the relevant questions in German— vomiting or no vomiting, et cetera. Then they gave me an anesthetic, only a so-called local anesthetic, and worked on me and sewed my head back together again. What I had thought was an enormous wound was only a laceration, after two days I was allowed to go back to Eugenia. Before, I had already been able to see my wreck at the police station right near the hospital. And to my amazement the police had been able to sketch an exact reconstruction of the accident. The Yugoslavian was one hundred percent responsible, and this was also stated in the report. The person who had kept screaming *Idiota!* as he ran away was his wife, who to her misfortune was a nurse at the hospital and, as I learned later, was instantly fired from her job in the nursing service because instead of helping me she had run away with her husband. I was sorry about this, but there was nothing I could do about it. My Herald was a lump of metal, I walked around it several times and I thought about how I'd only driven it for seven hundred and fifty miles. A shame. With a white turban around my head and my aunt and all her considerable luggage I set off on the journey home to Vienna. Not at all depressed, because finally I had by some miracle escaped with my life, but still very disappointed over the end to my automobile happiness. At the Heller car dealership they put me in touch with a Nobel-class lawyer who lived in the Heinrichshof. He would pursue the case with his renowned thoroughness, the lawyer said, while the people whom I told about my accident thought I'd never see so much as a cent from Yugoslavia, it was well known that they never paid a thing in such cases, even when the other party was one hundred percent guilty. I got angry that I'd taken on this, so it seemed to me, very expensive lawyer, I was furious over my own stupidity. Now I've not only lost my Herald, but I'm also paying the lawyer, who was set up like a prince in three or four enormous rooms with a direct view of the Opera. I'm really stupid, I told myself, a completely unrealistic person. *Amras* was typeset and I walked around the city of Vienna rather despondently. Nothing gave me pleasure, I missed my Herald, and I suddenly had a feeling again that I'd reached the end. Unlucky people never escape their bad luck, I said to myself, meaning me. It was unjust, but understandable. Every few days or weeks a letter from the lawyer fluttered in, in which he told me, always in the same words, that he was pursuing my case with the greatest diligence. Every time such a letter arrived, I went wild. But I no longer had the courage to go and see the lawyer and tell him he should give up the case, I was afraid of the enormous costs. In the Wertheimstein Park and the Zögernitz Casino I read the galleys of *Amras*. The book works, it's romantic, something born of a young man who'd been reading Novalis for months. After *Frost* I'd thought I could never write anything again, but then, by the sea, I'd sat down and *Amras* was there. It was always the sea that saved me, I only needed to go to the sea and I was saved. One morning another of those letters from the lawyer fluttered in and I was ready to tear it up. The content of the letter was different. Come to my office, the lawyer wrote to me, I have been able to settle your case with the fullest satisfaction. The Yugoslavian insurance people had actually agreed to all my lawyer's demands, without any restrictions whatever, it should be noted. Not only was my car replaced, but I also received damages. And a so-called compensation amount for my clothing that was unbelievably large. The lawyer had not admitted I was wearing nothing but cheap trousers, a shirt, and sandals, he'd stated I was in an expensive suit and most costly underwear. I left the lawyer's office in the highest order of happiness, naturally. I bought myself a new Herald and drove it very frequently to Yugoslavia, which had shown itself to be so correct and indeed so very generous to me in my misfortune. I've written all this, because, as you can see, it's all tied up with the dividing into thirds of the Julius Campe Prize. In the most self-evident way.

The Austrian State Prize for Literature

I received the Austrian State Prize for Literature in 1967 and I must say right away that it was a question of the so-called Small State Prize, which a writer receives only for a particular piece of work and for which he has to nominate himself, by submitting one of his works to the relevant Ministry of Culture and Art, and which I received at an age in which under normal circumstances one no longer receives it at all, namely in my case the late thirties, because it has become customary to award this prize to twenty-year-olds already, which is quite right—so it was a matter of the so-called Small State Prize and not the so-called Large State Prize, which is given for a so-called life's work. No one was more surprised

than I was that I'd been awarded the Small State
Prize, for I hadn't submitted a single one of my
works, I would never had done that, I had no idea
that my brother, as he later admitted to me, had
handed in *Frost* at the great entrance to the Ministry
of Art and Culture on the Minoritenplatz on the last
day submissions were being accepted. I was the
opposite of delighted with the news that I was getting the prize, a mass of young people had received
this prize before me and, in my eyes, had fully deval-
ued it. But I didn't want to be a spoiler and I also
took the prize because I would receive it thirty years
to the day after my grandfather received it in 1937.
This point was what made me tell the Ministry I
would accept the prize with the greatest pleasure. In
reality I had a queasy stomach at the idea that as an
almost forty-year-old I would have to accept a prize
which should be offered to twenty-year-olds, and in
particular I had a very strained relationship with
my country, as I do today to an even greater degree,
and my most strained relationship of all was with
our Ministry of Culture and Art, which I despised
from close and firsthand knowledge, the first place
in my contempt being held by the then-incumbent
Minister. In my youth I had been in this Ministry
more than once to procure a so-called Foreign Travel

Grant, this was in my twenties, for I wanted to travel around a great deal almost all the time and I had no money for it, and the Ministry had given me such a grant two or three times, I know for sure I have them to thank for two trips to Italy. But every time I came out of the Ministry I cursed its officials and the way the Ministry dealt with people like me, and I also had learned to hate it for many other reasons I don't want to broadcast here. I found the officials there self-important and dull-witted, and they didn't know what I was talking about when I talked with them and they had the worst imaginable taste in any and all fields of our art and culture. In short, now I had to come to grips with the fact that one day in the new year I had to collect the State Prize for *Frost* which my brother for whatever absurd reason had handed in at the porter's lodge on the Minoritenplatz. I felt it a humiliation that they were now throwing the so-called Small State Prize at my head, but I didn't want to make a scene and my brother had succeeded in convincing me that the right thing to do was to accept the prize without protest. So now I had to go to this very Ministry and allow these very people to hang a prize on me when I heartily despised both them and it. I had sworn never again to set foot in the Ministry in which only dull-wittedness and hypocrisy reigned, but now I was in this straitjacket my brother had stuck me in. Several newspapers had played up the announcement that I was getting the prize as if it were the Big Prize while it was the to-me-humiliating Small Prize. I choked on this fact and went around for weeks with this choking in my throat. But I didn't want to expose myself by refusing it, for then everyone would have accused me again of being arrogant and megalomaniacal, and incapable of real self-judgment. But much as the thought of having to go to the Ministry and collect the Small Prize made me choke, I kept being saved by the fact that even the Small Prize carried a sum of money, twenty-five thousand schillings back then, that, being in debt way over my head, I urgently needed. It was these debts my brother was thinking of when he allowed himself the outrageous liberty of handing in my *Frost* at the porter's lodge of the Ministry. So, I admit, because of the prize amount of twenty-five thousand schillings, I came to terms with the prize, with all the horrible, repellent things that necessarily came with the prize, I still despised the prize only as long as I didn't think about the twenty-five thousand schillings, if I thought about the twenty-five thousand schillings, I bowed to my fate. The whole time I thought about having or not having the twenty-five thousand schillings, and moreover my brother was right when he said I should just go and collect the prize without any fuss and refrain from making any comments. Secretly I was thinking that the jury was indulging itself in sheer effrontery in giving me the Small Prize when of course the only thing I felt absolutely prepared to accept, should the question arise, and it had already been raised, was the Big Prize and not the Small, that it must be giving my enemies on this jury a fiendish pleasure to knock me from my pedestal by throwing the Small Prize at my head. Did they, I thought, really think *I* personally would have competed for the Small Prize and offered myself up with open eyes and in full awareness to their aesthetic dilettantism? It was possible they thought I had handed over *Frost* at the porter's lodge of the Ministry myself. That is probably the case, that's how they were and they were incapable of thinking otherwise. The people who spoke to me about the prize all assumed I had naturally been awarded the Big Prize and each time I was faced with the embarrassment of saying to them that the one in question was the Small Prize which every scribbling asshole had won already. And each time I had to explain to people the difference between the Small Prize and the Big Prize, and when I did, I had the impression they simply didn't understand me anymore. The Big Prize, I kept repeating, was for a so-called life's work and one gets it closer to old age and it's awarded by the so-called Cultural Senate which is made up of all those who have previously won this Big State Prize and there wasn't just the Big State Prize for Literature but also for the so-called Fine Arts and for Music, et cetera. When people asked me who had already won this so-called Big State Prize, I always said, All Assholes, and when they asked me the names of these assholes I listed a whole row of assholes for them and they'd never heard of any of them, the only person who knew of them was me. So this Cultural Senate, they said, is made up of nothing but assholes because you say that everyone in the Cultural Senate is an asshole. Yes, I said, the Cultural Senate is full of assholes, what's more they're Catholic and National Socialist assholes plus the occasional Jew for window-dressing. I was repelled by these questions and these answers. And these assholes, people said, elect new assholes to their Senate every year when they give them the Big State Prize. Yes, I said, every year new assholes are selected for the Senate that calls itself a Cultural Senate and is an indestructible evil and a perverse absurdity in our country. It's a collection of the biggest washouts and bastards, I always said. And so what is the Small State Prize? they asked and I replied the Small State Prize is a so-called Nurturing of Talent and so many people have already won it you can no longer count them, and now I'm one of them, I said, for I've been given the Small State Prize as a punishment. Punishment for what? they asked and I couldn't give them an answer. The Small State Prize, I said, is a dirty trick if you're over thirty and as I'm almost forty it's a huge dirty trick. But I said I'd sworn to come to terms with this huge dirty trick and I had no thoughts of declining this huge dirty trick. I'm not willing to give up twenty-five thousand schillings, I said, I'm greedy for money, I have no character, I'm a bastard too. People didn't give up, they drilled down. They knew exactly where to drill to drive me crazy. They met me in the morning and congratulated me on my prize and said it really was high time for me to get the State Prize for Literature, and then made a pregnant pause. I then had to explain that my prize was the Small State Prize, a dirty trick not an honor. But no prizes are an honor, I then said, the honor is perverse, there is no honor in the world. People talk about honor and it's all a dirty trick, just like all talk about any honor, I said.

The state showers its working citizens with honors and showers them in reality with perversities and dirty tricks, I said. My aunt always had the highest opinion of our state and of states in general, her husband had been a senior state official, and she behaved as if I'd received an honor when the news was published in the papers that I was to receive the State Prize. So I had to explain to her too that this was the Small Prize and not the Big Prize and once again I tried to explain the exact differences between the two prizes and at the end of my explanation I said neither the Small nor the Big State Prize was worth anything, both prizes were a dirty trick and it was a low thing to accept either one of them, but I was sufficiently lacking in character to accept the prize because what I wanted was the twenty-five thousand schillings. My aunt was disappointed in me, until then she had had too high expectations of me. I shouldn't accept the prize, she said, if what I thought was what I said. Yes, I said, I think what I'm saying and I'm going to accept the prize all the same. I'm taking the money, because people should take every penny from the state which throws not just millions but billions out the window on a yearly basis for absolutely nothing at all, every citizen has a right to it and I'm not a fool.

We had a worthless government that used every
means to play to the gallery and hold on to power
even when the state was going to the dogs, of course
I would take twenty-five thousand schillings from a
state like this. Base or not, lacking character or not, I
said. My aunt accused me of inconsistency. She was
not to be persuaded of my point of view. I don't
believe, I said, that I'm lacking character if I take the
prize amount from people I bottomlessly loathe and
despise, quite the opposite. To compensate for the
humiliation of being given the Small State Prize I
should be able to take a trip, so many countries even
in Europe were still unknown to me, the twenty-five
thousand schillings would give me the opportunity
to go to Spain, for example, where I'd never been. If
I don't take the money for myself and use it to pay
for a trip, I said, it will be thrown to some useless
person in revenge, who causes nothing but damage
with his creations and poisons the air. The closer
the day of the prize-giving came, the more almost
unbearably sleepless nights I had. What possibly
had really been dreamed up by idiots as an honor, to
me, the more I thought about it, was a despicable
act, a beheading would be putting it too strongly
but even today I feel the best description of it is a
despicable act. All the twenty-year-old and twenty-

two-year-old and twenty-five-year-old fashionably dressed writers of radio plays I met on the street were winners of the State Prize. They behaved as if I had just been consecrated by them. It rankled. Moreover their perspective was right. My *Frost* had not received a single positive review anywhere in Austria, on the contrary, it was given a takedown in every single Austrian newspaper as soon as it appeared, not in the appropriate places, the way I'd imagined, but at the bottom, be it left or right, where worthlessness and contempt have made their home forever. I was angry, my anger had the absolute limitlessness born of lack of self-control, but in the end I kept asking myself if all these people might not be right. Perhaps I really wasn't worth any more than the value they put on me! I forbade myself to go on brooding about it. Time is pitiless. It was then too. The morning of the prize-giving had arrived. On this occasion too I was supposed to give a speech, but I'm no speaker and I can't give any speech whatever, I've never given a speech because I'm incapable of giving one. But I had to give a speech, it's a tradition that the writer, who receives this prize at the same time as a painter and a composer et cetera, gives a speech that was characterized in the Ministry's invitation as a speech of thanks. But as always, when I was supposed to give a speech, no speech came to me, in this instance too I had spent weeks thinking about what I would say, what my speech would be, but I had reached no result. What was there to say on such an occasion except the words *Thank you!* which still stick in the throat of the person who has to say them and sit in his stomach for a very long time. I found no theme for a speech. I wondered if perhaps I should go into the world situation, which, as always, was bad enough. Or the underdeveloped countries? Or the neglect of health care? Or the terrible state of our schoolchildren's teeth? Should I say something about the state per se, or art per se or about culture in any way at all? Should I even say anything about me? I found it all repellent and queasy-making. Finally I sat down with my aunt at the breakfast table and said, I can't give a speech, I have no idea what to say in a speech. I haven't thought of a theme, I haven't thought of anything. Maybe after breakfast, said my aunt, and I thought yes, maybe after breakfast and I ate breakfast and ate breakfast but still nothing came to me. Now I had my suit for best occasions on, the anthracite-colored single-breasted one, and I'd tied my tie and was struggling to swallow the last mouthfuls of breakfast and still I didn't have even the trace of an idea for a speech, suddenly I had absolutely nothing in my head except a feeling of fear, I was afraid of what was ahead of me, if I couldn't know precisely what I was afraid of, I feared something perverse, something unlawful, something unjust, something utterly embarrassing. My aunt was all ready to go, once again she looked very elegant and I admired her. If only I'd declined, and now didn't have to go to the Ministry, I said. And then, at the peak of my despair, I sat down at the table in the window of my tiny room and typed a few sentences on my machine. Again it was no speech, as they were requiring of me, again it was only a few sentences that I had in my head. Only a few sentences, I said to my aunt, and I was embarrassed to read her these newly minted sentences. I also wouldn't have had time to, for we had to leave, we caught a taxi on the corner of the Obkirchergasse and the Grinzinger Allee and drove into the city. This journey was the journey to the scaffold. The prize ceremony was taking place in the so-called Audience Chamber of the Culture and Art and Education Ministry. When we arrived, all the so-called honored guests were already there. Only the Minister was still missing, Herr Piffl-Perčevič, a former Secretary of the Provincial Agricultural Department in Steiermark with a walrus moustache, who had been summoned straight from his position in Steiermark to become Minister of the Ministry of Culture, Art, and Education. By his friend in the party, who'd just become Chancellor. I had always loathed this Piffl-Perčevič, for he was incapable of uttering a sentence correctly and it may be that he understood something about Steiermarkian calves and cows and Upper Steiermarkian pigs and Lower Steiermarkian hotbeds, but he understood absolutely nothing about art and culture although he talked about art and culture everywhere nonstop. But that's something else. The Minister with his walrus moustache came into the Audience Chamber and the prize ceremony could begin. The Minister had taken his seat in the first row where the prize candidates were sitting, five or six of them excluding me. This prize ceremony also began with a piece of music, it was a piece for strings and the Minister listened to it with his head tilted to the left. The musicians weren't in good shape and they stumbled in a lot of places, but on such occasions there's no expectation ever of accurate playing. It pained me that the musicians stumbled over all the best passages in the piece. Finally the piece came to an end and the Minister was handed a piece of paper by his secretary with what was probably a text the secretary had written, whereupon the Minister stood up and went to the lectern and gave a speech. I no longer remember the content of the speech, it introduced all the prizewinners, some of their biographical details were read out and some of their works were named. Naturally I couldn't know if what the Minister had read out about my co-winners was correct, what he said about me was almost all wrong and crude and manufactured out of thin air. He mentioned, for example, that I had written a novel that takes place on an island in the South Seas, which in that moment when the Minister shared this information was absolute news to me. Everything the Minister said was wrong, and evidently his secretary had confused me with someone else, but it didn't make me more upset, because I'm used to politicians always talking nonsense on such occasions and things that have been conjured out of midair at best, why should it be any different with Herr Piffl-Perčevič. But what did wound me deeply was the announcement by the Minister that I, and I can still hear every word in my ear, *was a foreigner born in Holland,* but who *had already been living among us for some time* (i.e., among the Austrians, of whom Minister Piffl-Perčevič did not consider me one). I was amazed at my calm as I listened to the Minister. One shouldn't hold their provinces against provincials, but when they appear in public with Herr Piffl-Perčevič's unrivaled arrogance, one should try not to let it slide. Now I had the opportunity and I didn't let it slide. A literally indescribable arrogance had displayed itself on the dull-witted, totally insensible, and unmusical face of the Cultural Minister as he proclaimed to the audience who I was. But probably even in this case nobody but my friends had any idea that the Minister was scattering nothing but dull-witted falsifications about me around the room. He felt nothing, he read out his secretary's brainless inanities in his natural monotone, one false statement after the other, one vulgarity after the next. Did I need this? I asked myself while the Minister was speaking if it wouldn't have been better not to come. But this question no longer made any real sense. I sat there and couldn't defend myself, I couldn't just jump up and say to the Minister's face that what he was saying was all nonsense and lies. I was tied to my chair by invisible cords, condemned to immobility. This is the punishment, I thought, now you have your reckoning. Now you've made yourself one of them, the people sitting in this hall listening with their hypocritical ears to his Holiness the Minister.

Now you belong to them, now you're one of the pack that's always driven you mad and you've avoided having anything to do with your whole life. You're sitting there in your dark suit taking blow after blow, one brazen lie after another. And you don't move, you don't jump up and box the Minister's ear. I told myself to stay calm, I kept saying to myself, *calm, calm, calm,* I said it over and over again until the Minister was done with his arrogant outrages. He would have deserved having his ears boxed, but what he got was tumultuous applause. The sheep were applauding the God that fed them, the Minister sat down amid the deafening clapping, and now it was my turn to stand up and go to the lectern. I was still shaking with rage. But I hadn't lost my self-control. I took the piece of paper with my text out of my jacket pocket and read it out, possibly in a trembling voice, it could be. My legs were shaking too, not surprisingly. But I hadn't got to the end of my text before the audience became restive, I had no idea why, for my text was being spoken quietly by me and the theme was a philosophical one, profound even, I felt, and I had uttered the word *State* several times. I thought, it's a very calm text, one I can use here to get myself up out of the dirt without causing a ruckus because almost no one will understand it, all about death and its conquering power and the absurdity of all things human, about man's incapacity and man's mortality and the nullity of all states. I hadn't even finished my text when the Minister leapt to his feet, bright red in the face, ran at me, and hurled some incomprehensible curse word at my head. He stood before me in wild agitation and threatened me, yes, he came at me with his hand raised. He took two or three steps, then an abrupt about-turn, and he left the hall. He rushed to the glass door of the Audience Chamber without any of his attendants and slammed it with a loud bang. This all took place in a matter of seconds. Hardly had the Minister single-handedly and above all furiously hurled the door of his Audience Chamber shut behind him than there was chaos in the hall. That is, first, after the Minister had slammed the door, there was a moment when embarrassed silence reigned. Then the chaos broke out. I myself had no idea what had happened. I had had to allow one humiliation after another to be heaped on me and then I had read out what I thought was my harmless text whereupon the Minister had gotten angry and left the hall in a rage and now his vassals were coming for me. The entire mob in the hall, all people who were dependent on the Minister, who had grants or pensions and above all the so-called Cultural Senate, which probably attends every prize ceremony, all of them rushed after the Minister out of the hall and down the broad flight of stairs. But all these people rushing away after the Minister didn't rush away after the Minister without first giving me a dirty look, as I was apparently the cause of this embarrassing scene and the sudden wrecking of this ceremony. They cast their dirty looks at me and rushed after the Minister and many of them didn't stop at dirty looks, they also waved their fists at me, most of all, if I remember correctly, the President of the Cultural Senate, Herr Rudolf Henz, a man then between seventy and eighty, he rushed at me and waved his fist and then chased after the Minister with the others. What have I done? I asked myself, suddenly left standing with my aunt and two or three friends. I wasn't conscious of having done anything wrong. The Minister hadn't understood my sentences and because I had used the word *State* not in a subservient way but in a highly critical context, he had leapt to his feet and attacked me and had run out of the Audience Chamber and down the broad staircase. And everyone else, with the meager exceptions already mentioned, had rushed off after him. I can still hear the way the Minister slammed the door to the Audience Chamber shut, I have never heard anyone bang a door that loudly. So there I stood and didn't know what to say. My friends, three or four, not more, and my aunt had moved over to me and had no answer either. The whole group turned toward the buffet that was still flanked by two waiters provided by the Sacher or the Bristol, gaping with shock, and wondered what was going to be done with the totally untouched spread. It'll go to an old age home, I thought. The Minister cold-shouldered you, not vice versa, said one of my friends. It was well said. He cold-shouldered everyone, I said. The Minister slammed the door to the Audience Chamber so hard, I thought, the panes must have given way. But when I investigated the door to the Audience Chamber, it turned out that not one pane was broken. It had only sounded as if the panes in the door to the Audience Chamber had broken. The newspapers next day wrote about a scandal that the writer Bernhard had provoked. A Viennese newspaper, which called itself the *Viennese Monday,* wrote on the front page that I was a bug that needed to be exterminated.

The Anton Wildgans Prize*

Anton Wildgans, like Weinhaber, is a Hölderlin of the Vienna suburbs who fits the soul of the people to a T. The prize that is named for him is funded by an industrial association that has its headquarters on the Schwarzenbergplatz in Vienna in a magnificent palace of the later nineteenth century. A week before I was to receive the Austrian State Prize, the president of the industrial association, Mayer-Gunthof, long since dead, informed me that the relevant jury had decided to give me this year's prize, which is to

---

* Anton Wildgans (1881–1932), poet and playwright, author of dramas of earnest social criticism, became the director of the Burgtheater in 1930. A vocal defender of Austria's independence against the National Socialists' plan to annex Austria to Germany.

say the prize for 1976. The president ended his letter with the customary formula that he was extremely pleased to be able to share this news with me. At the given moment, I receive the invitation to the ceremony. The prize is endowed with twenty-five thousand schillings. I didn't give any thought to Wildgans, for I estimated him lower than my writer friends on the jury who, for whatever absurd reason, had hit upon the idea of awarding me the Wildgans Prize for 1976. In Austrian acting schools, it's customary for the students to have a constant diet of Wildgans and above all they're already learning a passage from *Armut* for the entrance exam and they spend their waking minutes reciting Wildgans poems and when it's a question of holding some highly official state occasion, be it in the Burgtheater or in the so-called Josefstadt or even in some ministry, someone is sure to reach for something by Wildgans. The dilettante's conception of Austrian poetry finds its ideal in Wildgans, as in Weinhaber, and practices it wherever there is a ceremony to be held, even today. What people admire in Wildgans is not only what they think of as his exceptionally sincere poetic art but, more importantly, the fact that he was once the director of the Burgtheater. What I myself always admired about Wildgans was his trombone-playing son, who was a musician of absolute genius and was among the most promising composers of his generation. But I don't want to talk about Wildgans here, I want to talk about the prize that bears his name. A few days before the ceremony for the State Prize took place in the Ministry on the Minoritenplatz, the invitation reached me for the prize-giving in the Industrial Association, on a grandiose piece of letterhead printed by the famous firm of Huber & Lerner on the Kohlmarkt, and on which it was announced that Minister Piffl-Perčevič would be the special guest of honor. If, I thought, I want new storm windows to replace the old ones on my house which are almost totally rotted, I have to accept the prize, and so I had decided to take the Wildgans Prize and take myself off to the Löwenhöle Salon on the Schwarzenbergplatz. I mostly thought that one should take money when it's offered and no one should waste time fussing around over the how and the where, all these reflections are nothing but total hypocrisy and so I ordered the storm windows from my local carpenter, the savings on heating costs will be considerable, I thought. No sensible person says no to twenty-five thousand schillings out of a clear-blue sky, whoever offers money has money and it should be taken from him, I thought. And the Industrial Association should be ashamed of funding a prize for literature with a mere twenty-five-thousand-schilling award, when they could fund it with five million schillings right there without even noticing it, but from their perspective, I thought, they're valuing literature and literary figures quite accurately and I even was surprised at their estimate of literature and the literary figures who created it. I would have taken twenty-five thousand schillings from anyone, even the first person I met on the street. No one reproaches a beggar on the street for taking money from people without asking where they got the money they're giving him. And it would have been utterly absurd to ask the Industrial Association, of all bodies, to actually have thoughts about their Yes or No, it would have been laughable. When I add the Industrial Association's twenty-five thousand to the twenty-five thousand for the State Prize—both shamelessly low amounts for such purposes, I thought, the state should be as embarrassed as the Industrial Association, for they award literary prizes in amounts that would be a poor monthly salary for a middle-ranking municipal employee—that makes fifty thousand and with that I really could do something. The state awards a prize that's no more than a shoddy pay packet and the Industrial Association does the same and both of them thus reveal themselves to the world, which totally fails to notice how vulgar and perverse this is. The Industrial Association with its millions or rather billions uses the giving of a shoddy prize sum of twenty-five thousand schillings to elevate itself to the lofty status of a truly exceptional Maecenas of Art and Culture and is even praised for this in every newspaper, instead of being denounced for their meanness with no regard for the consequences. But my intention wasn't to denounce, merely to report. The Wildgans Prize was to be awarded a week after the State Prize. As per the invitation. But after, as I have reported, the State Prize ceremony exploded and the Minister slammed the door to the Audience Chamber in his Ministry with a huge bang and stormed out, the Industrial Association on the Schwarzenbergplatz suddenly lost their guest of honor for their planned Wildgans Prize award ceremony, for the Minister in his role as guest of honor had abruptly informed the Industrial Association that he did not wish to be the guest of honor at a ceremony whose central focus would be *a certain Herr Bernhard,* he declined and the Industrial Association was left standing. But because the Industrial Association no longer had their chief attraction, namely the Minister, at their disposal, they no longer wanted the writer Bernhard, with whom they had merely tried hypocritically to set themselves up as a Maecenas on a national scale. And what did the Industrial Association do? They canceled the entire ceremony and re-sent the same invitation cards they had had printed by Huber & Lerner on the Kohlmarkt and sent out two weeks before, not as *in*vitations now but as *dis*invitations. The celebration they had announced two weeks before would not take place and was *canceled,* it said on what I called the *disinvitation cards,* still in the same Hispano-Hapsburgian fashion of court announcements from Huber & Lerner, all in black and gold. I was sent this disinvitation minus any further communication about the whys and wherefores, just like the other invitees, and I was sent the prize certificate, also minus comment, in a shabby tube for printed matter that came by regular mail. Luckily they had also sent me, without comment, the twenty-five thousand schillings, a sum which in my view was completely inadequate for this whole tawdry outrage.

Shortly afterward I met Gerhard Fritsch, a member of the jury and my friend until then, in the Museum

Café at the very table where Robert Musil used to sit, and asked him if after this disgusting business with the Industrial Association he was going to protest their behavior and step down from the jury and resign his seat. But Fritsch had no intention either of protesting or of stepping down from the jury. He had three wives and a whole bunch of children with these wives to take care of, he said, and could not indulge himself in any such protest even if it was self-evident to me, or any such self-evident resignation (self-evident to me, that is) from the Wildgans Prize jury. As a father of many children and provider for three female money-pits he felt really sorry for me and asked me to show him consideration in a tone that was repellent. The poor man, the malleable, pitiable, wretched man. Not long after this conversation Fritsch hanged himself from the hook on his apartment door, his life, which he'd bungled with no help from anybody, had closed over his head and extinguished him.

The Franz Theodor Csokor Prize

Franz Theodor Csokor was a philosopher and dramatist and the author of a book titled *As a Civilian in the War in the Balkans,* which I had discovered in my grandfather's library, and he was for many years the president of the P.E.N. club and a friend of my grandfather's whom he deeply honored, and for many years he stayed in the tavern on the Wallersee that belonged to relatives of mine and in which I ran around when I was three and four and five and six and even when I was seven and eight, without having the faintest idea who the two gentlemen, Franz Theodor Csokor and Ödön von Horváth, were who were staying below me in the large rooms embellished with their Empire and Biedermeier furniture and a whole series of valuable late-eighteenth-century pieces and magnificent stucco work and their view onto the woods. Csokor and Horváth, the two friends who wrote the majority of their plays and novels in my relatives' tavern, supposedly played with me on the wooden floors downstairs in the lower taproom and took me on walks to the lake, but I myself can no longer recall this. My grandfather often took walks with Csokor and Horváth, as I know. In my relatives' tavern was a large room on the second floor where plays were put on all year round and perhaps this was the right atmosphere for the two playwriting friends, I still remember the mountains of brilliantly colored theatrical costumes under the roof and also a piece that was put on in the room in which a naked man tied to a post was whipped, for what reason I don't know, but I can still see the scene quite clearly, it made a horrible impression on me, it was a political drama. Maybe Csokor and Horváth were inspired by this stage, it's probable. I only met Csokor one time later on, in Salzburg, what the occasion was I no longer recall, but I do remember that he sat with the novelist George Saiko and me on the terrace of the restaurant in the fortress and talked uninterruptedly about my grandfather, all things that had gone on that were unknown to me. He loved my grandfather, for the way he talked about my grandfather is the way one only talks about someone one loves. Because I myself loved my grandfather like no one else on earth, I was happy to listen. For Saiko, a thoroughly self-important and egocentric type, and then a famous man, these descriptions of Csokor's were almost unendurable, sometimes he tried to interrupt Csokor, but Csokor wouldn't allow himself to be interrupted. *This man,* said Csokor, *was once the Director of the Albertina in Vienna,* and this information impressed me enormously. After the end of the meal Csokor, who was already an old gentleman at that time was tired but Saiko wasn't tired and said goodbye to Csokor and said to me that as I was young and therefore naturally not yet tired, I should show the city of Salzburg to him, Herr Saiko, who wasn't tired either. I had no idea at that moment what catastrophe was ahead of me. Csokor had barely taken his leave before Saiko, who had written the novel *The Man in the Reeds,* started to explain to me what a novel is. So we walked through the city in the burning heat and Herr Saiko told me nonstop what a novel is. I led him from one little street to the next, from one church to the next, but all he talked about was the novel, he stuffed me full of his theories about the novel, completely obliviously, he had absolutely no idea that his incessant articulation of his theories was already giving me a headache and I hated literary theories more than anything in my life, but most of all I hated so-called theories about the novel, particularly when promulgated by fanatical theorists like Saiko, who started by extinguishing all feeling for the material in the listener by talking at full volume. Herr Saiko talked and talked and talked for four hours about what a novel is and never stopped citing major or minor novelists and sometimes he said he'd misspoken, it wasn't Joyce who'd said this or that, it was Thomas Mann, not Henry James but Kipling. My admiration that the man had once been the Director of the Albertina shriveled to the barest minimum over the course of this four-hour lecture, yes I suddenly despised this speechifier, I hated him and I kept thinking the whole time how I could get rid of him. But it was five hours, as I remember, before Saiko, having worn himself out, suddenly realized that he had more or less annihilated me with his lecture and said goodbye. I was too tired to catch my breath. I traveled to Venice overnight, as I recall, I woke up there to a beautiful morning and ran to St. Mark's Square. But who suddenly spread his arms wide when he saw me coming, Herr Saiko! Naturally I wasn't shocked by this absurdity, but willed myself to accompany Saiko to a restaurant near the Bridge of Sighs to eat cheese and olives and drink red wine. Herr Saiko had now stopped his perorations and was a pure pleasure-lover. He was going to Ancona that evening with his wife, he said, and pointed to a white ship in the background. But I didn't want to talk about Herr Saiko but about Franz Theodor Csokor whom everyone who knew him had to love. After I returned from Venice I found a letter from Csokor in which he informed me that the P.E.N. club had just elected me a member! Unanimously! By ballot! Now I had a real mess. As with every other association in the world, I had no desire, naturally, to be a member of the P.E.N. club either. How to say this to the lovable old gentleman who wrote the Austrian national play *3 November 1918* without wounding him? I had nothing against the P.E.N. club fundamentally, even today I don't really know what it is, but on no account did I wish to be a member, I had always hated associations and societies, and of course literary associations most of all. This is the reason I only recently resigned from the so-called Darmstadt Academy which I'd never signed up for and thirty years ago I also resigned from the Socialist Party, which I had actually signed up for not long before, I didn't and don't like parties and societies. So I sat down and wrote Csokor that I was conscious of the enormous honor of being elected to the P.E.N. club by ballot, as he'd told me, but that I couldn't overturn my principle of never becoming a member of another association and it was because of this very principle that I couldn't even be a member of an association of which he, Csokor, was president. I felt dreadful after mailing the letter. I did not receive an answer. Eventually Csokor died, and then so did Herr Saiko, after he'd received the Big Austrian Prize for Literature four or five weeks before his death and had explained to me (three days before his death) on a streetcar ride from Döbling to the First District that when buying shoes you should never buy them before four in the afternoon because it's only around four in the afternoon that the foot takes on the correct and proper consistency for shoe-buying. Whenever I'm reminded of Saiko, who, as I mentioned, was the author of *The Man in the Reeds,* the first thing I think of is his lecture about never buying shoes before four in the afternoon and I have retained something of that lecture even today, and his four-hour lecture on what a novel is comes in second. But I have a real affection for both of these dead men today, whether they wrote the most incredible masterpieces of Austrian literature or not I come back to them, because my encounter with them is intimately connected with the awarding of the Franz Theodor Csokor Prize. When I won the prize which is dedicated to Csokor's memory, the people who gave me the prize assumed that of course I was a member of the P.E.N. club. When I said no, of course I wasn't a member of the P.E.N. club and told them my P.E.N. club story, they were very disappointed, for maybe they would never have given it to me as a nonmember. When I received the prize, in the P.E.N. club palace in the First District near the Minoritenkirche, presented by Piero Rismondo, the only one of the critics in Vienna who had time for my plays, I was in the process of being exposed to a particularly savage wave of personal attacks in the Austrian newspapers. Why, I don't know. At any rate, it was definitely thumbs down. So the award gave me a real boost. Herr Rismondo, that subtle, cultivated man from Trieste, could not know that his words of approval lifted up a man who had been laid flat, that his prize speech was received greatly like music to the ears of someone who'd almost been broken. It was at this time that my *Shooting Party* and *The President* and Peter

Handke's *A Leap in the Dark* were being produced
and this, it is thought, caused a deputation of the so-
called Cultural Senate of the state, led by their president, the writer Rudolf Henz, to the Minister of
Culture in his Ministry, in the form of a resolution
demanding that the Minister should kindly inter-
vene with the directors of the Burgtheater to ensure
that Bernhard and Handke would no longer be produced, Bernhard and Handke being, as one could
read daily in the Vienna papers, bad writers whereas
he, Henz, and his fellows in the Cultural Senate were
good writers. The scribblers who were all suckling
on the bosom of the state were full of themselves!
Every newspaper reported this hair-raising event
without a single critical comment. This is only one
example of the literary mood that prevailed in the
country back then against me and Handke. Not for
the first time, I wondered around then whether
prizes should be accepted or not. After the Julius
Campe Prize, the only one I accepted with a sort of
leap of joy, I had a constant empty feeling in my
stomach whenever there was a question of accept-
ing a prize, and my mind balked every time. But I
remained too weak in all the years that prizes came
my way to say no. There, I always thought, is a major
hole in my character. I despised the people who

were giving the prizes but I didn't strictly refuse the prizes themselves. It was all offensive, but I found myself the most offensive of all. I hated ceremonies but I took part in them, I hated the prize-givers but I took their money. Today I can no longer do it. Until you're forty, I think, but after that? That I didn't accept the prize money of eighteen thousand schillings attached to the Franz Theodor Csokor Prize, but had it donated to the care of prisoners in Stein,* was also no way out. Even actions like this, that have a so-called social aspect, are not free of vanity, self-prettying, and hypocrisy. The question simply no longer presents itself, the only answer is to decline all further honors.

* Famous Austrian prison.

The Literary Prize of the
Federal Chamber of Commerce

The literary prize of the Federal Chamber of Commerce was the last prize I received, together with Okopenko and Ilse Eichinger, for the book *The Cellar* in which I describe my time as an apprentice salesman in the Scherzhauserfeld estate on the edge of Salzburg, and from the beginning I associated this prize not with my activities as a writer but with my activities as an apprentice salesman and during the ceremony, which had no connection whatever to the city of Salzburg but which took place nonetheless in the old Schloss Klessheim on the Saalach, the only thing spoken of by the gentlemen of the Federal Chamber of Commerce who had given me the prize was Bernhard the apprentice salesman and never Bernhard the writer. I felt tremendously well among the worthy gentlemen of the merchant class and the whole time I spent with these gentlemen I had the impression I didn't belong to literature, I belonged with the merchants. In singling me out and inviting me to the Schloss Klessheim they brought back vividly a time when I was an apprentice that had served me well my whole life, supplying the population of Scherzhauserfeld with groceries under the care of my master Karl Podhala. Walking up and down in front of the Schloss before the ceremony, the autumnal mood in the park was extremely conducive to my reconstruction of my life as an apprentice, I was once again the sixteen- or seventeen-year-old in a gray work coat pouring vinegar and oil into the narrowest of necks of bottles from a height of almost two feet without a funnel, like a virtuoso, something that nobody in the shop could imitate. I carried the hundred-and-seventy-five-pound and two-hundred-and-twenty-pound sacks from the storeroom into the shop in the cellar and at midday on Saturdays I knelt on the floor to wash it while my boss did the day's accounts. I opened the concertina barrier in the morning and closed it at night and in between it was my constant wish to serve the people of

Scherzhauserfeld and my master. A few weeks ago
when I went into one of the hundreds of branches of
Austria's largest chain of shoe shops, in one of the
neighboring villages, there hanging on the wall were
the rules for the conduct of apprentices I'd formu-
lated in *The Cellar*. The management had copied
these rules from my book and had them printed up
for their apprentices by the hundred. I stood in the
shop, where I'd wanted to buy myself some gym
shoes, and read my own rules on the walls and for
the first time in my literary career I had the feeling
that I was a useful writer. I read my rules several
times without letting on who I was, and then I
bought the pair of gym shoes I wanted and went out
of the shop and felt the deepest satisfaction. *The
Cellar* describes my about-turn in the Reichenhaller-
strasse, the moment one morning when instead of
going to high school I went to the employment
office to look for a place as an apprentice, and what
followed. Now in the park of Klessheim I had the
time and the peace before the prize-giving ceremony
to yield to the melancholy that had overtaken me
here in this park and I gave myself over to it happily.
First alone, then with friends, I walked along the
familiar walls, these were the walls, I thought, I'd
slipped along at the end of the war, to cross the

heavily guarded, forbidden border in the twilight. That was thirty-five years ago. Hitler had wanted to create a residence for himself in this Schloss. But where is Hitler? In this Schloss Presidents Nixon and Ford spent the night more than once, as did the Queen of England. Now the Schloss was home to the Federal Chamber of Commerce's hotel school, which is world famous. And the students at this hotel school had cooked an absolutely magnificent meal for all the participants in the ceremony, the prizewinners and everyone else, and laid a beautiful table. The prize-giving took place in the hall, opened by a quartet or a quintet. Merchants are economical with words and the President of the Federal Chamber of Commerce had accordingly kept himself brief. All three prizewinners were treated, one after the other, to a eulogy by a university professor, in which the attempt was made to base the awarding of the prize. I had, according to mine, found a totally new form of autobiography. When the checks were handed over, mine was for fifty thousand schillings. The group of musicians brought the morning celebrations to an end. As was appropriate in such a setting, everyone took their places at a table decorated with little handwritten place cards. And now, to my surprise, I was sitting right next to the President of the Salzburg Chamber of Commerce, Haidenthaller, who told me once I'd sat down that it was he who had tested me at my oral apprentice salesman's exam. He could remember the event of more than thirty years ago exactly. Yes, I said, I remember too. President Haidenthaller had a soft voice and I liked his way of speaking. My aunt was seated opposite me and my Salzburg publisher on my left. While my neighbor on my right, President Haidenthaller, fell silent once for a long moment, my publisher whispered into my ear that Haidenthaller was terminally ill, and had only another two weeks to live, cancer, my publisher whispered into my ear. When Herr Haidenthaller turned back toward me, there was naturally a new dimension to the conversation. Now I was much more careful with the distinguished gentleman who came, as I knew, from one of the oldest families in Salzburg, a dynasty of mill owners, and it turned out later that he was even related to me. He had read *The Cellar,* he said, nothing else. He had asked me about several sorts of Chinese tea in my apprentice salesman's exam and I had given the correct answers. That question was always the hardest, he said. The event was as relaxed as could be, it's the way merchants are. Today the apprentices didn't need to be able to specify so many kinds of tea at their exam, nor so many kinds of coffee, around a hundred kinds of tea and around a hundred kinds of coffee, a hundred kinds of tea and coffee all different in their look and smell, the trickiest question in the exam, said President Haidenthaller. Naturally all through the rest of the conversation with him I was thinking about what my publisher had said to me, about the imminent and inevitable death of my table companion. The whole time I was thinking what I might say to my former examiner in the apprentice salesman's exam to make this lunch as enjoyable for him as possible. We exchanged some experiences we'd had in our common hometown of Salzburg, named a whole series of names we both knew, laughed a few times, and I noticed my table companion even guffawed once. Did he know he was about to die? Or was the whole thing a nasty rumor? Conversation with someone you know is about to die is not the easiest. Deep down I was glad when the table was cleared and all the participants said their good-byes. The prize-giving had begun so beautifully and ended so sadly. In the days following the ceremony in Klessheim I went daily to my coffee-house in Gmunden to read the papers, and first of all always the column that contains the death announcements. Two weeks had already gone by and the name Haidenthaller had not appeared in print, neither in the deaths column nor on the obituaries page. But on the fifteenth or sixteenth day Haidenthaller's name was in the paper, in large letters and bordered in black. My publisher had only been off by one or two days, he hadn't been spreading a rumor. I sat in the coffeehouse and observed the seagulls in front of the window as they greedily pecked the old retired women's chunks of bread out of the stormy waters of the lake and screeched off and suddenly I heard everything again that Herr Haidenthaller had said to me at the table in Klessheim, with the greatest reticence and distinction that he owed to his position and his ancient family. Without the Prize of the Federal Chamber of Commerce I would not have seen Herr Haidenthaller again and I wouldn't know as much today as I know about my own forebears as I did after my meeting with him, he knew my people well.

The Georg Büchner Prize

I received the Büchner Prize in 1970, when the so-called Student Revolution of 1968, having subsided as a merely romantic and thus totally unsuccessful dilettantish revolt, had already entered history as an unfit attempt at a revolution, alas. The frivolousness of this protest had finally led to a result that was the opposite of what was intended and thus an intellectual catastrophe and a sad awakening. The people pushing this movement with one eye on the French did not, as they intended, bring back to Germany the good, the best, the spirit that feared no consequences, they only drove it out for a long time with their dilettantism which had nothing revolutionary about it but was merely a fashion stolen from the

French, as we can now see. The general attitudes now reigning in Germany are obviously more depressing than they were before the events of 1968. It was no movement in the sense of Büchner's and his gang's movement, only a perverse game with the intellectual boredom that has been a tradition in Germany for hundreds of years. The Büchner Prize is linked with a name I had conjured only with the deepest respect for decades. For my work in directing, at the end of my studies at the Mozarteum I chose, without needing much reflection, alongside Kleist's *The Broken Pitcher* and Thomas Wolfe's *Mannerhouse*, Büchner's *Leonce and Lena*. But because I've never been able to be very articulate about any of the things I've loved most in my life, I've also almost never said anything about Büchner. The speech that the Germany Academy required of me for being awarded the Büchner Prize had to go against this inarticulacy and so it never took shape. On the contrary, I was certain that I had no right to express myself in any way about Büchner on the podium in Darmstadt, indeed, I was certain that the name Büchner should not even cross my lips if possible, and in this I was successful, for I only said a few sentences in Darmstadt and these had nothing to do with Büchner. We are not allowed to keep talking endlessly about those we consider great and to hitch our own pitiful existence and inadequacies to these great ones with all our efforts and our clamor. It is customary that people when they get a Kant plaque or a Dürer Prize give long speeches about Kant or Dürer, spinning dull threads that extend from the great ones to themselves and squeezing their brains over the audience. This way of proceeding doesn't appeal to me. And so I only said a few sentences in Darmstadt which had nothing to do with Büchner, though everything to do with me. Finally I had no need to explain Büchner, who needs no explaining, at most I needed to make a short statement about myself and my relationship to my surrounding world, from the center of my own world which is also, of course, for as long as I live, the center of the world itself for me, and must be so, if what I say is going to be true. I'm not reciting a prayer, I thought, I'm taking a standpoint which can only be *my* standpoint, when I speak. In short, I spoke few sentences. The listeners thought that what I said was an introduction to my speech, but it was the whole thing. I gave a short bow and saw that my audience wasn't pleased with me. But I hadn't come to Darmstadt to make people happy, but only to collect the prize, which came with ten thousand marks and with which Büchner had nothing to do, since he knew nothing about it himself, having died so many decades before there was any idea of funding a Büchner Prize. The so-called German Academy of Language and Poetry had everything to do with the Büchner Prize, while Georg Büchner himself had nothing. And I thanked the German Academy of Language and Poetry for the prize, but in truth I was only thanking them for the prize money, for when I went to Darmstadt I no longer had any relationship to the so-called honor that such a prize was supposed to signify, this honor and all other honors had already become suspect to me. But I had no cause to share my views with the Academy, I packed my bag and went to Darmstadt with my aunt because I wanted to spoil myself and my aunt with a beautiful trip through Germany after a long barren period at home in the country. The gentlemen of the Academy couldn't have been friendlier and I had several pleasant conversations with them which contained nothing dangerous, for I didn't want anything to disrupt my trip through Germany. I had to take the prize ceremony upon myself as a curiosity and Werner Heisenberg, who was being honored in the same ceremony with a prize for scientific writing, had also said to me more than once how curious the ceremony was, what the famous critic from the *Süddeutsche Zeitung,* Joachim Kaiser, who was also getting a prize then, thought, I can't say, he was inscrutable. After the distribution of the prizes, when I said to Joachim Kaiser, who was sitting next to me in the front row, that my prize certificate was a third larger and thus also heavier than his, embodying the different relevant weights of the prizes, he made a face. But I have to say that afterward in a nearby cellar restaurant he impressed me with his knowledge of musicology, in the face of such astonishingly concentrated richness I had nothing to contribute. The city of Darmstadt gave me a lunch, to which some of my friends also came, I was allowed to provide names and they were all invited. During lunch when my aunt told her neighbor at the table, Minister Storz, that it wasn't only Büchner who had his birthday that day, it was hers too, she was seventy-six, one of the gentlemen of the city got to his feet and went out. Somewhat later he returned carrying a bouquet of seventy-six roses. Here I have to say that the main reason I went to Darmstadt was to make a beautiful birthday for my aunt, for she was born, like Georg Büchner, on October eighteenth. Of course it wasn't the only reason but it was the main reason. At the end of the meal my aunt and I signed our names in the Golden Book of Darmstadt. The newspapers covered the tripartite prize, albeit from different perspectives and with wildly different resources, in ways that pretty much matched my own opinions. The articles are there to be read. The jury of the German Academy, from which I have since resigned, because they elected me a member without my knowledge, and I couldn't defend this, is answerable for my being voted the winner of the Büchner Prize, not me.

SPEECHES

Speech at the Award Ceremony for
the Literarure Prize of
the Free Hanseatic City of Bremen

Honored Guests,

I cannot follow the fairy tale of your town musicians; I don't want to tell a story; I don't want to sing; I don't want to preach; but it's true: fairy tales are over, the fairy tales about cities and states and all the scientific fairy tales, and all the philosophical ones; there is no more *world of the spirit;* Europe, the most beautiful, is dead; this is the truth and the reality. Reality, like truth, is no fairy tale and truth has never been a fairy tale.

Fifty years ago Europe was a single fairy tale, the whole world a fairy-tale world. Today there are many who live in this fairy-tale world, but they're living in a dead world and they themselves are dead.

He who isn't dead lives, and *he doesn't live in fairy tales; it's no fairy tale.*

I myself am no fairy tale and I do not come from a world of fairy tales; I had to live through a long war and I saw hundreds of thousands die, and others who went on right over them; everyone went on, in reality; everything changed, in truth; in the five decades during which everything turned to revolt and everything changed, during which a thousand-year-old fairy tale gave way to *the* reality and *the* truth, I felt myself getting colder and colder while a new world and a new nature arose from the old.

It is harder to live without fairy tales, that is why it is so hard to live in the twentieth century; it's more that we *exist,* we don't live, no one lives anymore; but it is a fine thing to *exist* in the twentieth century, to *move,* but to *where*? I know I did not emerge from any fairy tale and I will not enter any fairy tale, this is already progress and thus already a difference between then and now.

We are standing on the most frightening territory in all of history. We are in fear, *in fear of this enormous material that is the new humanity,* and of a new knowledge of our nature and the *renewal* of our nature; together we have been only a single mass of pain in the last half century; this pain today is *us;* this pain is now our spiritual condition.

We have a wholly new system, a wholly new way of seeing the world, and a wholly new, truly most outstanding view of the world's own surroundings, and we have a new morality and we have new sciences and new arts. We feel dizzy and we feel cold. We believed that because we are human, we would lose our balance, but we haven't lost our balance; we've also done everything to avoid freezing.

Everything has changed because it is we who have changed it, our external geography has changed as much as our internal one.

We make great demands now, we cannot make enough great demands; no era has made such great demands as ours; we are already megalomaniacal; because we know we *cannot* fall and we *cannot* freeze, we trust ourselves to do what we do.

Life is only science now. The science of the sciences. Now we are suddenly taken up with nature. We have become intimate with the elements. *We* have put reality to the test. Reality has put *us* to the test. We now know the laws of nature, the infinite High Laws of nature, and we can study them in reality and in truth. We no longer have to rely on assumptions. When we look into nature, we no longer see ghosts. We have written the boldest chapter in the book of world history, every one of us has written it *for himself* in fright and deathly fear and none of us of our own free will, nor according to his own taste, but following the laws of nature, and we have written this chapter behind the backs of our blind fathers and our foolish teachers, behind our own backs; after so much that has been endlessly long and dull, the shortest and the most important.

We are frightened by the clarity *out of which our world suddenly is born,* our world of science; we freeze in this clarity; but we wanted this clarity, we evoked it, so we cannot complain now that the cold reigns and we're freezing. The cold increases with the clarity. This clarity and this cold will now rule us. The science of nature will give us a greater clarity and will be far colder than we can imagine.

Everything will be clear, a clarity that increases and deepens unendingly, and everything will be cold, a coldness that intensifies ever more horribly. In the future we will have the impression of a day that is endlessly clear and endlessly cold.

I thank you for your attention. I thank you for the honor you have shown me today.

Speech on the Occasion of
the Awarding of the Austrian State Prize

Honored Minister, honored guests,

There is nothing to praise, nothing to damn, nothing to accuse, but much that is absurd, indeed it is all absurd, when one thinks about *death.*

We go through life impressed, unimpressed, we cross the scene, everything is interchangeable, we have been schooled more or less effectively in a state where everything is mere props: but it is all an error! We understand: a clueless people, a beautiful country—there are dead fathers or fathers conscientiously without conscience, straightforwardly despicable in the raw basics of their needs . . . it all makes for a past history that is philosophically significant and unendurable. Our era is feebleminded, the demonic in us a perpetual national prison in which the elements of stupidity and thoughtlessness have become a daily need. The state is a construct eternally on the verge of foundering, the people one that is endlessly condemned to infamy and feeblemindedness, life a state of hopelessness in every philosophy and which will end in universal madness.

We're Austrian, we're apathetic, our lives evince the basest disinterest in life, in the workings of nature we represent the future as megalomania.

We have nothing to report except that we are pitiful, brought down by all the imaginative powers of an amalgam of philosophical, economic, and machine-driven monotony.

Means to an end when that end is destruction, creatures of agony, everything is explained to us and we understand nothing. We populate a trauma, we are frightened, we have the right to be frightened, we can already see in the background the dim shapes of the giants of fear.

What we think is secondhand, what we experience is chaotic, what we are is unclear.

We don't have to be ashamed, but we are nothing, and we earn nothing but chaos.

In my name and in the name of those here who have also been selected by this jury, I thank all of you.

Speech at the Awarding of
the Georg Büchner Prize

Honored guests,

What we are speaking of here is unfathomable, we are not properly alive, our existence and suppositions are all hypocritical, we are cut down in our aspirations at the final, fatal conclusion of our lethal misunderstanding with nature, into which science has led us and abandoned us; appearances are deadly and all the hundreds and thousands of hackneyed words we play with in our heads in our loneliness, the words that are recognizable to us in any language and within any context as the monstrous truth revealed in monstrous lies, or better, monstrous lies revealed within a monstrous truth, the words we say and write to one another and the ones we dare to suppress, the words that come from nothing and go to nothing and serve nothing, as we know and keep secret, the words to which we cling because our impotence makes us insane and our insanity makes us despair, these words merely infect and ignore, blur and aggravate, shame and falsify and cloud and darken everything; by mouth and on paper they abuse by means of their abusers; the very character of words and their abusers is an outrage; the spiritual condition of words and their abusers is that of helplessness and catastrophic good cheer.

We say we're putting on a performance in a theater that will last for all eternity . . . but the theater in which we're prepared for everything and competent in nothing is, from the time we're able to think, a theater of ever-increasing speed and lost shorthand . . . it is absolutely a theater of the body—and secondarily of spiritual angst and thus of the fear of death . . . we don't know whether we're dealing with tragedy or comedy, or comedy for the sake of tragedy . . . but all of it deals with the terrible, with misery, with mental imbalance . . . we think we should keep quiet: he who thinks destroys, annuls, metes out disaster, corrodes, demolishes, for thinking is consistent with the dissolution of all ideas . . . we are made up (and this is history and the spiritual condition of history) of anxieties, bodily anxiety, spiritual anxiety, and the anxiety about death that drives creativity . . . what we reveal is not identical with what is, being shattered is something else, existence is something else, we are something else, the unendurable is something else, it isn't illness, it isn't death, those relationships are quite other, as are those circumstances . . .

We say we have a right to what's right and just, but we only have a right to what's not right and what's unjust . . .

The problem is to get work done, which means advancing over all one's inner resistance and evident mindlessness . . . and this means advancing over myself and the bodies of dead philosophers, over all of literature, all of science, all of history, everything . . . it is a question of one's spiritual constitution and one's spiritual concentration, of isolation and distance . . . of monotony . . . of utopia . . . of idiocy . . .

The problem is always to get work done while thinking that work will never get done and nothing will ever get done . . . The question is: to go on, heedless of the consequences, to go on, or to stop, to call it a day . . . it is the question of doubt, of mistrust and impatience.

I thank the Academy, and I thank you for your attention.

On My Resignation

The election of Scheel, the former President of the Federal Republic, as an honorary member of the Academy for Language and Poetry, was for me the final and definitive reason to separate myself from this Academy for Language and Poetry, which in my view has nothing whatever to do with either language or poetry and the justification for whose existence must self-evidently be denied by every thinking person with a good conscience. For years I have wondered about the point of this so-called Darmstadt Academy and I have always had to tell myself that the only point consists in an association which in final analysis was founded merely for the self-image of its preening members, comes together twice a year to indulge in self-adulation, and there, after traveling in luxury at the expense of the state, eats splendid high-class dinners and drinks high-class wines in good Darmstadt hotels for almost a week while beating around the bush, literarily speaking. If one poet or writer is laughable and hard for human society to bear, how much more laughable and ridiculous is a whole horde of writers and poets and people who think they're writers or poets, all in a heap! At bottom, all these previous prize-winners come together in Darmstadt at the state's expense, after a year of impotence and mutual loathing, to spend another week in Darmstadt boring one another to death. Writers' chitchat in the hotel lobbies of provincial Germany is the most distasteful thing imaginable. The stink is however even stinkier when it's being subsidized by the state. The whole contemporary steaming subvention racket stinks to high heaven! Poets and writers should not be being subsidized, and certainly not by an Academy that is itself subsidized, they should be left to themselves.

The Academy for Language and Poetry (the most absurd title in the world!) gives out an annual *Yearbook,* and maybe this has a point? But every *Yearbook* prints so-called essays which are dust covered before they're even typeset and have nothing to do with either language or poetry, or anything to do with the creative, because they come from the clogged typewriters of thick-witted gasbags, or as we'd say in Austria, heedless busybodies. And what else is in the *Academy Yearbook,* aside from these stale effusions? A long list of all the possible and impossible obscure honors that these intellectual earthworms have received in the preceding year. Whom does this interest, aside from the earthworms themselves? Plus also, not to be forgotten, a hypocritical "list of the deceased," with embarrassing obituaries playing a sort of Academy poker game of the dead, each one raising the stakes of cringe-making stupidity against the others. A shame that this *Yearbook* is printed on such expensive paper that it's no good for heating my stove in Ohlsdorf. Every time the mailman leaves this load with me, I have the greatest difficulty with it.

But, people will say, the Academy for Language and Poetry (the Büchner Prize should be awarded to its inventors for this term alone!) gives out the Büchner Prize, the so-called most-admired literary award in all Germany. I don't see why this obscure Academy has to award the Büchner Prize, for nobody needs an Academy to hand out this award. Certainly not an Academy for Language and Poetry which is a conceptual and linguistic curiosity as its title indicates, nothing more. Seven years ago exactly, when I was elected to the Academy, I didn't think about it further or take it seriously. It was only gradually that the dubiousness of this Darmstadt Academy dawned on me, and I literally took this dubious entity seriously for the first time at the moment when I read that Herr Walter Scheel had been elected to this Academy, and I promptly resigned. If Herr Scheel is entering, I thought, I can exit at the same time.

I wish the Academy for Language and Poetry, which I consider the most dispensable institution in Germany and indeed the entire rest of the world, and which most certainly is more noxious than useful to those poets who are real poets and those writers who are real writers, the very best with Herr Scheel. Whenever one of its members dies, the Darmstadt Academy (for Language and Poetry!) always automatically sends out a black-bordered death-announcement card with an identically worded obituary text (whose language and poetry could furnish cause for argument). Maybe I'll live to experience the day when they send out a card memorializing not the death of some honorable member, but their own.

Thomas Bernhard was born in Holland in 1931 and grew up in Austria. He studied music at the Universität Mozarteum in Salzburg. In 1957 he began a second career as a playwright, poet, and novelist. The winner of the three most distinguished and coveted literary prizes awarded in Germany, he has become one of the most widely translated and admired writers of his generation. His novels published in English include *The Loser, The Lime Works, Correction, Concrete, Woodcutters, Gargoyles, Wittgenstein's Nephew,* and *Frost;* a number of his plays have been produced off-Broadway, at the Guthrie Theater in Minneapolis, and at theaters in London and throughout Europe. The five segments of his memoir were published in one volume, *Gathering Evidence,* in 1985. Thomas Bernhard died in 1989.

Carol Brown Janeway's translations include Bernhard Schlink's *The Reader,* Jan Philipp Reemtsma's *In the Cellar,* Hans-Ulrich Treichel's *Lost,* Zvi Kolitz's *Yosl Rakover Talks to God,* Benjamin Lebert's *Crazy,* Sándor Márai's *Embers,* Yasmina Reza's *Desolation,* Margriet de Moor's *The Storm,* and Daniel Kehlmann's *Measuring the World* and *Fame.*

A NOTE ON THE TYPE

This book was set in Celeste, a typeface created in 1994 by the designer Chris Burke. He describes it as a modern, humanistic face having less contrast between thick and thin strokes than other modern types such as Bodoni, Didot, and Walbaum. Tempered by some old-style traits and with a contemporary, slightly modular letterspacing, Celeste is highly readable and especially adapted for current digital printing processes, which render an increasingly exacting letterform.

Composed by Creative Graphics,
Allentown, Pennsylvania
Printed and bound by Thomson Shore,
Dexter, Michigan
Designed by Soonyoung Kwon